Reset!

A blueprint for a better life

ROSALYN PALMER

Reset!
A Blueprint for a Better Life

First published in 2018 by
Panoma Press Ltd
48 St Vincent Drive, St Albans, Herts, AL1 5SJ UK
info@panomapress.com
www.panomapress.com

Cover design by Neil Coe
Artwork by Karen Gladwell

ISBN 978-1-784521-40-0

Dedication

To Mum and Dad. You always told me that life
was full of endless possibilities. Thank you.

Thanks to Anne, Hayley, Jo, Kath and Linda
– my personal editorial team – for your
invaluable input.

Testimonials

'Rosalyn has lived a life, where on the outside, it has looked amazing and enviable yet on the inside it has been a struggle. The life lessons and wisdom she has gained in her interesting and connected life has taught her that changing your attitude begins as something you do and then becomes who you are. I met Rosalyn in the 90s when she came to me for therapy and changed her life. We have stayed in touch and remained friends all these years and I knew her experiences and her wisdom could make an excellent therapist. That is why I invited her to my very first RTT training and why she is now one of my top trainers and therapists. She has followed my training, and now helps others to live happy full lives free from pain. This book fuses her journey with the therapeutic advice she offers and anyone who reads it will discover that it works. I'm proud of how she has taken what I've taught her and shared it with others and I know that I can always count on her to do wonderful work both with me and for me.'

Marisa Peer, world-renowned speaker, celebrity therapist, Rapid Transformational Therapy trainer and best-selling author

'I saw far too much of my own personal situation in this book, and I'm sure I won't be alone. The good news is, this book provides solutions and a way forward. Wish I'd read it years ago!'

Deborah Garlick, founder of Henpicked.net

'I am an advocate for people taking complete control of their own lives and destinies, from their health, to their job, to their personal life. We are experiencing a paradigm shift right now in healthcare, and by taking control of your health and life, you can succeed past your own dreams, and be the healthiest you can be, personalised to you. Rosalyn used a perfect Sylvester

Stallone quote "Life is not about how hard of a hit you can give... it's about how many you can take and still keep moving forward". In her new book *Reset!*, Rosalyn outlines how you can take charge of your life, overcome challenges, and live the life you want – all on your own terms.'

Robin Farmanfarmaian, professional speaker, investor, and entrepreneur and Author of *The Patient as CEO*

'In the years I've known, and worked with, Rosalyn, I've seen her steer through challenges and difficulties with integrity and courage. This journey and her hypnotherapy skills have created a blueprint for a life of purpose and a career now spent freeing others from pain. Having lived the experiences she gained the insights needed. This book shares the journey and offers practical insights and exercises for anyone who wants to improve their life and find their joy. It's more than just a book; it's a toolkit you will want to revisit. I fully endorse it.'

Wanda Goldwag, Chair & Non-Executive Director (including Chair Legal Ombudsman)

'I have read many books on self-development and self-love and spirituality. I live my life by constantly facing challenges and growing. I feel the fear and face it with courage and optimism. That's why my husband Al and I overcame adverse conditions together to become three-times World Freestyle Skydive Champions and six consecutive times British Freestyle Skydive Champions. Each time we jump, and work together, it feels like a Reset button has been pressed. This book really encapsulates that message. It is about how even the difficult times in our lives can make us take stock, stop, connect with a greater force and make us stronger and better and happier. Having spent time with Rosalyn I know this to be true of not only what she does but also how she lives.'

Pixie MacLeod-Hodgson, British & World Champion Freestyle Skydiver

Acknowledgements

Thank you to Marisa Peer and her bespoke Rapid Transformational Therapy (RTT) training. Many of my references to the workings of our minds, therapeutic understanding and methodologies are as a direct reference to my training in RTT.

Contents

Introduction

This book is for any woman or man who is living a life that looks great from the outside. Perhaps you have the lovely house, lifestyle, career and trappings of success. However, like my archetypal client, 'Burnt-out Barbara', you lie awake at night with your whirligig mind in overdrive as yet another day at work sees you stave off a panic attack by bolting to the toilet where, after 10 minutes of deep breathing, you are able to compose yourself. Perhaps, like one of my high-flying female executive clients, it will only be when your young son brings home a bright crayon drawing from school entitled 'My Mummy' that depicts you, mobile to your ear and briefcase in hand, that your heart will nearly break and you decide that enough is enough. You long for rest, for ease, to feel at one with yourself, to discover your purpose. To dare to feel joy and connection and be intimate with your partner, family, friends and yourself.

Barbara has shelves of self-help books already. She relies on therapies, complementary treatments and distractions such as expensive weekends away, quality food and fine wines and shopping to balance her broken life.

I understand her and these issues deeply. This was the blueprint of my life when I ran an award-winning London UK PR company and had all the trappings of success, but was exhausted and addicted, wanting the merry-go-round to just stop, and it did stop. I thought I had got out in time, dodged a bullet by selling my PR company, selling my large London house and moving with my family to the Bahamas. This is where it all imploded.

Coming through this, I was repeatedly offered the heartfelt advice of, "You must write a book about your life", and eventually I started to nurture the idea.

My life had taken so many twists and turns, moving me from comprehensive school kid who lived in her early years above her parents' shop, to leading my PR success story in London, to recovering from cancer on an Out Island in the Bahamas, a return as a jobless single mother to the UK, bereavement, reinvention, remarriage, divorce, reinvention again and then an invitation to train in hypnotherapy.

I added hundreds of hours of additional training and became a Rapid Transformational Therapy leading trainer, with clients worldwide. I considered a book title of 'The Accidental Therapist', but as my book flowed from my heart and mind onto the page, I wanted to signpost it for the women and men that I truly desired to reach. To share my story and then give those life lessons context from a therapeutic point of view. Most importantly, to offer a blueprint of proven, easy-to-follow advice for how to get through even the most life-threatening and soul-destroying of issues and emerge happier, stronger and with a sense of purpose.

This is my journey. These are my experiences. This is what I have learned. This is what I know now and wish I had known years ago. I hope it inspires you, guides you and resets your life for the better.

CHAPTER ONE

Stop living the wrong life

"All men dream, but not equally. Those who dream by
night in the dusty recesses of their minds, wake in the day
to find that it was vanity: but the dreamers of the day are
dangerous men, for they may act on their dreams with
open eyes, to make them possible."

T. E. Lawrence

My Personal Story

It was at the Cardiff Millennium Stadium that my love affair
with Madonna hit the rocks. I'd been a material girl, desperately
seeking something, and the soundtrack to my life until that night
in 2008 had been provided mostly by Madge. Sadly, she stepped
out on stage late, gave a lacklustre 45-minute performance, only
connected with the audience at *La Isla Bonita* and then, without
an encore, left. My adoration had left with her.

Perhaps I was growing old or growing up, but I was fed up. She
had sung *Hung Up* and I'd momentarily felt a bit better. I left
feeling betrayed. Yet the lyrics to her song *Nobody Knows Me*
would not stop playing in my head – on repeat. "I've had so
many lives/Since I was a child/And I realise/How many times
I've died/Nobody, nobody knows me/Nobody knows me."

That is how I felt in my life. Misunderstood. Lonely. Like I kept
living the 'wrong life' and was an actress in a play I had not realised
I had auditioned for. This pattern had been playing out for longer

for longer than I could remember. While struggling through depression and using Cognitive Behavioural Therapy (CBT) to get off the meds, I realised I had felt like that forever. I had come through so many life events and losses that my CBT therapists marvelled at my ability to be merely depressed and disconnected without going the whole hog and developing Dissociative Identity Disorder as a way of coping with the many challenges I faced. My therapist wanted to do a case study. I wanted to feel happy. I wanted to feel alive. I wanted to sleep well at night without Zopiclone and have a sense of centredness during the day that wasn't courtesy of Citalopram.

So many people, especially baby boomer women: the 'squeezed middles', feel like this. Perhaps you have felt it many times, as I have done in my life. Just when I think I have it all figured out, life has a habit of throwing a new curve ball. Now however, those balls just sail on past me or I catch them, use them or throw them back. I am walking, talking evidence that no matter what happens, you can get your life back. What's more, with these life lessons and transformational therapy techniques, you can go way beyond just 'Recovery' mode and re-envision and re-engineer not just a good life, but an outstanding life full of passion, joy, balance and fun. A consciously planned life where you grow continuously and with ease, due to having a toolkit of emotional and physical 'fixes' that can make you bulletproof. In other words, you can Reset Your Life. Again and again.

Back in the early 80s, I hitchhiked around Ireland with my boyfriend at the time. We were studying Irish literature. He had a penny whistle and would sit by whichever road in the middle of nowhere we were stranded on and screech out a terrible tune. We had a backpack each and very little money. It did not matter, as we managed to hitch lifts at each stage of the journey. Often the drivers were not going to where we had planned, but we went anyway. There were no Airbnbs then or mobile phones and a night in a field full of cows never appealed. My favourite lift came when we were deep in County Clare, far from anywhere and getting a tad concerned about dusk falling. A battered old van came into view. I flagged him down. He was charming. I said where we were headed and asked if we could hitch a ride. The priceless reply came: "Jesus, if you want to go there then you don't want to be starting from here."

This is how life or the thought of changing it often feels. You say to yourself: "It would be OK if only I didn't have to start from here", but you have to. That is the only place you can start. Even if it is so painful and disappointing that you would rather just not even think about it. In fact, the more painful your current location in life is, the more you need to think about it – not for a long time, as I'm sure you have already been suffering for far too long and it is compromising your health, wealth and welfare. No, just long enough to work out what is causing the pain so you can create new and immediate strategies to minimise the discomfort while you pack for your new journey. A journey to the new continent of you, because if a tanker changes course in an open sea, to the naked eye a change of only one or two percent is unnoticeable, but the resulting course often takes that ship not just to a different country, but a different continent.

This is the first step in your journey to resetting your life course to the New Continent of You.

Rejection and how your brain is hardwired to avoid it

Our deepest fear as human beings is the fear of rejection. Reject a baby and it will die physically or fail to thrive emotionally. Think of nature and it's the same. Picture a David Attenborough documentary as he speaks in hushed tones and we watch the baby wildebeest crying for its mother after crossing the river. It has been separated from its mother and will die. Think of the small cuddly panda cub who is rejected by a mother more intent on eating bamboo. Unless hand-reared, it too will perish.

So rejection cuts the deepest. Rejection by a parent or sibling as you grew up. Rejection at school; perhaps you were bullied as you were 'different'. Rejection in your much hoped-for career so you've had to settle at your job and hate every day. Rejection in love. Having your heart broken so badly that you feel unable to breathe. It is horrible but it is survivable.

Some people seem able to bounce back from rejection time and time again. Type into Google: 'Celebrities who have come back from rejection' and thousands of examples appear. Madonna and U2 were famously passed over by record producers who didn't feel that they were 'ready' before they signed to greatness. J.K. Rowling had so many rejection letters prior to finding a publisher for *Harry Potter* that she just filed them in a box in her attic. When asked to get them out she said no, but shared some of the rejection letters she received while writing under the pen name of Robert Galbraith. The kindest came from Constable & Robinson who advised her to take a writing course and gave helpful hints on how to pitch to a publisher before concluding that they had, "reluctantly come to the conclusion that we could not publish it with commercial success". The first two Robert Galbraith books have reached sales of 1.5m copies across print, e-book and audio books.

Today Sylvester Stallone is regarded as a hugely successful actor and can command tens of millions of dollars per movie, yet he was rejected over and over again. Due to his determination and clarity about what he wanted: to be an actor, he defied the odds. His slightly asymmetrical expression and slurred speech are due to the lower part of his jaw being paralysed. He was rejected over 1,000 times when auditioning as an actor because of this. Yet his mantra is:

"I take rejection as someone blowing a bugle in my ear
to wake me up and get going, rather than retreat."

Homeless and so broke he had to sell his beloved dog. He was inspired by a fight between Muhammad Ali and Chuck Wepner and the idea for his movie *Rocky* took root. He wrote it in one go. He then pitched it to agents with the caveat that he would play the starring role. After countless rejections, he even received an offer of $225,000 for the screenplay but with no deal on his acting role. He held out and finally was offered what he wanted, the lead role in his own movie, but for only $35,000.

The movie *Rocky* was released in 1976 and won three Oscars for best picture, best directing and best film editing. Sylvester Stallone was nominated for best actor. It has grossed over $225 million and spawned a further six movies in the franchise. Sylvester Stallone is a multi-millionaire, happily married to a beautiful wife and has starred in countless other movies.

"Life is not about how hard of a hit you can give...
It's about how many you can take and
still keep moving forward."

— **Sylvester Stallone**

In one of Fred Astaire's first screen tests, an executive wrote: "Can't sing. Can't act. Slightly balding. Can dance a little."

Change the word 'celebrity' to 'businessperson' on the Google search and an even bigger list appears. Walt Disney was fired from the Kansas City Star because his editor felt he "lacked imagination and had no good ideas". Vera Wang failed to make the 1968 US Olympic figure-skating team. Then she became an editor at *Vogue*, but was passed over for the editor-in-chief position. She began designing wedding gowns at age 40 and today is a leading fashion designer, with a business worth over $1 billion. Thomas Edison's teachers told him he was "too stupid to learn anything". While developing his vacuum, Sir James Dyson went through 5,126 failed prototypes and his savings of 15 years. Prototype 5,127 worked. Today, Dyson is the best-selling bagless vacuum brand in the United States. Along with a knighthood, James has also amassed an estimated $4.9 billion, according to Forbes.

Are these bounce-back kids wired differently to you and me? No. They simply deal with rejection in a different way and it is more than just rolling with the punches. I used to say of myself, "I'm a Weeble: I wobble but I don't fall down" (this was the advertising mantra for the 70s toys 'Weebles' which had weighted bottoms so that if you tried to make them fall, they would not do so). I also hear at difficult times the strains of *Tubthumping ("I get knocked down but I get up again")* by Chumbawumba in my head. The trouble is that for most of my life I'd look like I was bouncing back and even doing so, but it was taking a huge internal emotional toll and this in turn affected me physically.

16

I needed more and more things to keep 'Weebling' and not falling down. Things such as alcohol, anger, sleeping tablets or allowing my subconscious to take charge of my appearance and keep my body thin and a size zero via being very good at bulimia. On the positive side, things such as acupuncture, massage, Ayurvedic medicine, psychotherapy, colonics, kinesiology, floatation tank therapy and more. All the latter were like plasters holding me together physically and emotionally. The former often just numbed the pain.

No, those who are truly bulletproof don't just bounce back from setbacks. They go a big step further and don't let criticism or nastiness in. They keep their self-esteem high. They love themselves no matter what.

They also stay present and listen intently. Most people convince themselves that they don't have a good memory, especially when it comes to names. Most often it is because when you are introduced to someone, you are busy thinking about what you are going to say or how you can create a good impression, and you never even hear or acknowledge their name. Remember, listen attentively as you have two ears and one mouth. Hack your brain by immediately making a connection from their name to something familiar that you can remember. When my new neighbour introduced herself as Aileen, I immediately watched and listened in my head to the iconic video of Dexy's Midnight Runners in denim dungarees singing 'Come on Aileen' and never had a problem recalling her name again. If you are momentarily struggling to recall something, say to yourself: "It will come back to me in a minute" and guess what, it will. Don't say: "God I have a memory like a sieve, I can never remember things" as that is the command to your brain. Like a genie in a lamp, your wish will be its command. These statements are commonly known as 'affirmations'.

The trouble is that it is often not the outside world or forces beyond our control that really cause us the most pain and knockbacks. It is our own inner dialogue. The biggest cause of depression is the harsh critical words we say to ourselves on a daily basis. "Oh there you go screwing it up again you idiot!" "I'm just a waste of space." "What was I thinking, I'm going to fail at this just like everything else." And so on. If you spoke to your friends, spouse, colleagues or children the way you speak to yourself, you would be very lonely.

Many of the mind patterns of words or mantras, rules and 'expected' behaviours are hardwired into us as children. The problem is, we continue to run on this outdated operating system and ignore the fact that new and amazing software has become available. It's like trying to install a new leading-edge app and each time the hidden code underneath the system overwrites it and takes it back to coding from years ago. You wouldn't put up with this on a computer or other gadget. Even if you bought a new piece of the same equipment, you would naturally expect it to be better than the one you owned before. For instance with a television – a clearer picture, better sound system, higher definition, easier to navigate, etc.

Yet we continue to run our minds and consequently our lives on outdated systems, and when we try to install new software such as a diet or new exercise regime, a year later have yo-yoed back to where we started and we wonder why. In fact, we go beyond that and add in the critical self-talk for good measure. "I can never make anything stick," or "I don't know why I bother,

I'm such a failure". What's worse, we then add in other outdated hardware that is still operating in us, without realising that these are thoughts and beliefs that we had to buy into when we had no other choice. The words from your well-meaning Gran: "You've inherited big bones from your dad's side, you'll never be thin", or your parents: "Money doesn't grow on trees", or the priest: "Money is the root of all evil" just play and play in your head and you are directed by them.

The list goes on. The insidious part is often that as you grow older, you are not even aware of these imposed beliefs. They are causing you to operate in a way that is at odds with what you now want, and because of this you feel frustrated, depressed, angry and at a loss as to how to fix it. For example, as was the case with me, your business is actually going well, but the more you earn, the unhappier you feel. Nothing brings you joy. If at an operating system level, you are hardwired to believe that money is the root of all evil, it's hardly surprising.

I launched my PR company with a £5k redundancy package, in my spare room, with my Basset Hound Rosie as the first member of staff. Three years later its turnover was £250,000 and we were getting noticed. My husband worked with me, we had several staff, nice offices and were winning pretty much everything we pitched for. Yet I was miserable. It all felt so burdensome. At night I couldn't sleep, as it felt like I had to keep spinning plates on poles. I was handling the UK PR for arguably now the world's greatest motivational guru, Tony Robbins, and going through his premier live course – Mastery University. I was in Maui, Hawaii, at Life Mastery, about to climb a 56ft telegraph pole, stand on the top and then jump off to catch a trapeze 12ft away to show that I could master my 'limiting beliefs', just as I had done by walking barefoot over burning coals the day before, but my body was having none of it. My mind was saying: "Climb the pole" but my body was saying: "No". I was immobilised. Then someone tapped me on the shoulder and said: "I can hypnotise you up that pole". Enter world-famous hypnotherapist, Marisa Peer. A few minutes later, I was at the top of a swaying pole, looking across the sea. Without thinking, I jumped off to catch the trapeze. I felt elated.

So when I realised I was not only feeling unhappy about the business, but that I was also self-sabotaging it, I went to see Marisa for a hypnotherapy session. I remember her rather amazing Courvoisier chair and her house in Fulham. I also remember standing on the street outside after the session, waiting for a cab and wondering if it had worked. Was I fixed?

In the next few months something amazing happened. We doubled our turnover and increased our profit margins. I was no longer the problem that was holding us back. I had discovered during my session with Marisa that although consciously I really wanted a successful business, I was subconsciously terrified about the potential wealth it would bring. I'd grown up a grocer's daughter living above the shop in my early years. Most Sundays, my father had a migraine and would be ill. My unseen operating rule No. 1 was that making money equalled working so hard that you will get ill.

I'd also been religious and spiritual, dipping in and out of organised religion and non-organised spirituality. It was the early 90s and Gordon Gecko told us that 'Greed is Good', but my hardwiring system told me otherwise. It told me that you had to sacrifice your soul for money. So, to make more money in the business would cost me my health. No wonder I was self-sabotaging. The subconscious mind will keep you alive at any cost. That is its primary function. That's why American outdoorsman Aron Lee Ralston was able to survive a canyoning accident in Utah in 2003 by amputating his trapped right forearm with a blunt pocketknife in order to survive. An act that is, under normal circumstances, utterly unthinkable. His subconscious knew that it was better to block out the pain and sacrifice an arm to keep the rest of him alive than to stay there until frostbite and hypothermia set in.

Your subconscious acts for survival and is hardwired at an early age. Hence someone who wants to lose weight and can't make it permanent goes to a slimming club, gets the certificates, the camaraderie and looks great for that special event they have been planning. Then 12 months later they are back at their old weight or even more. This makes them unhappy about how they look and who they are, so their sex life suffers, their health suffers and their internal talk is critical and harsh. They are so unhappy that they take to snapping at the kids and pushing their partner away. Everyone suffers and it is not their fault. It is the fault of their outmoded operating system, telling them: "You nearly died of diphtheria when you were two and everyone said that you needed to fatten up or that the cold would kill you. You can't get thin. It will kill you", or, "You hated it when the boys singled you out at school for being the flat-chested rake. When you developed breasts they paid attention. Don't get thin and rake-like again. No one will find you attractive".

You get the picture. What you need is a strategy to renegotiate with your subconscious. This can be facilitated by a therapist or hypnotherapy recordings, and you can start the self-help process through following the exercises.

Of course you could be very internally well adjusted, but a perfect storm of external circumstances just overwhelms you. Within a two-year period, my first unease started when I was faced with an inability to earn money in a foreign country, mourning my former 'me' based on the ego of my successful former career.

Then, in an 18-month period my father had a stroke, I developed breast cancer and my mother was diagnosed with terminal pancreatic cancer, necessitating hospital visits in the United States for me and flying 4,500 miles to visit my parents. We were living in the Bahamas and we moved to an Out Island for me to recover. With all this I found it a struggle to be a mum to two young boys in a very different culture, keep my marriage from falling apart at the seams and recover my health.

I nearly pulled it off until I discovered that much of the financial bedrock I had sacrificed my health to achieve was no longer there. Even in my darkest hours, I had consoled myself with the thought of, 'At least we have the money in the bank'. Divorce proceedings and moving back to the UK followed. Mum died shortly afterwards.

So let's face it, the external issues will come.

As Baz Luhrmann says in *Everybody's Free (to Wear Sunscreen)*

Don't worry about the future or worry; know that worrying
is as effective as trying to solve an algebra equation
by chewing bubble gum.
The real troubles in your life are apt to be things
that never crossed your worried mind.
The kind that blindsides you at 4 p.m. on some idle Tuesday.

Reset! A Blueprint for a Better Life

What is irrefutable is this: even if you don't think that any of your internal hardwiring will exacerbate your difficult life experiences, you darn well need to ensure that it is as bulletproof as possible. To be a Weeble that wobbles but does not fall down and does so while still maintaining a sense of calmness and optimism. The good news is that it is possible. I'm living proof, and by the end of this book you will have the tools and insight to do this and reset your life too.

Understanding is power. So let's gain a little more understanding at the outset to enable you to deconstruct and understand just what is making you feel unhappy and causing you pain presently.

The False sense of Fulfilment

There are societal pressures which are overwhelming us like never before. Social MEdia is all about the 'Edited ME'. 'Look at me having fun. Look at me looking perfect (it only took 35 selfies and a bit of retouching but I look fab).' 'Look at me and my fabulous life' scream the Facebook and Instagram posts.

We don't tend to post the photo of our self as we truly are first thing on a November morning when we have to force ourselves to get ready and go to work, the kids have lost their shoes again, the dog has been sick on the carpet and another bill has landed on the doormat. We stop that honesty and instead see our friend's Facebook post from their holiday in Bali as they look tanned and beautiful. The 'edited' her.

Back to Baz Luhrmann. *Do NOT read beauty magazines. They will only make you feel ugly.* Yes, to get you through the day after the morbid depression of the news, fuelled by the cheerful madness of some morning show DJ, you grab a magazine to read with your coffee to cheer yourself up. Sadly, by page 10 you feel utterly inadequate and empty, so you fill yourself up with a cake for now and then a quick purchase from the high street during your lunch. Yes, that's the solution you say to yourself at a subconscious or conscious level: "If I wear that top I saw in the magazine worn by that happy celebrity, my life will be so much better. I will buy happiness. It will fix me. It will fill me." Perhaps it will, for a few hours.

Pressures like this are crippling women and men of every age. Young girls are bombarded by over-sexualised images and young boys are watching so much porn that they have totally unrealistic expectations of what happens intimately between two people or how most women look naked.

So, when after countless cosmetic procedures people are still not happy, they turn to other things to fill them up. Just look at some celebrities. The pressure to look great and pretend life is fun all the time just breaks them. They sit in their massive houses and binge on food or alcohol or drugs and it is never enough. If you watch the documentary on the talented, but fragile Amy Winehouse, you will see her saying at a point when she is sober that doing a concert without drugs makes it all so boring. What she is saying is that she felt boring. Not enough. Not interesting for who she was. Not worthy, as she was uncomfortable with earning money for a talent that she didn't recognise and that was exploited by many around her.

Marilyn Monroe was the same. She was planning her divorce from Arthur Miller the day she married him. If you believe that love is not available to you, as Marilyn did having been placed for adoption as a baby and then fearing that men only wanted her for her looks, you know no other modus operandi than to plan a pre-emptive strike to end a relationship. In her subconscious mind, she believed that all her relationships were doomed to fail.

For most people the big issue is the pressure of work. You have to earn a living. How else will you survive or thrive? How will your children and significant others be provided for? After all, isn't this career what you worked hard for throughout school and university?

At its best, work fulfils many of our basic human needs. If you are familiar with Maslow's Hierarchy of Needs, you can see that at the very least work enables us to meet our Physiological Needs, enabling us to buy food, shelter and warmth plus the ability to rest. At the next level, work and money earned allow us to meet our Psychological Needs as we belong to a team or company and can make friends and connect. We can then gain prestige and feelings of accomplishment. If we are really lucky, we can even be self-actualised and reach our full potential, but I see countless patients who bash up against the invisible ceiling between the prestige and any feelings of being fulfilled, creative or free.

It is usually at this level where high flyers get their wings clipped. They have the job title, the huge salary and even the prestige with their photo plastered all over their company website. They can even be the 'Go-To' advisor for their area of specialty and even find some connection with their work colleagues or peers. This in and of itself can often be an issue. They can be bright, positive, driven and connected at work and then go home completely spent, with nothing left for their partner, children or themselves. They are living in a house of cards.

If this high flyer is a female, for example Theresa May or Hillary Clinton, for good measure they also get judged publically and cruelly on their looks and/or dress sense as if taking them apart in this fashion is going to make them better at their job. They are criticised if they are too feminine, as this is equated to weakness when in a position of power, and they are criticised as having become a 'ball breaker' or other derogatory term if they tap into their masculine side too much. This creates havoc in heterosexual relationships, as women feel the need to be more assertive or male and their testosterone levels rise. Nature creates natural balance in close relationships, so often their partner's testosterone will lessen and his estrogen levels will rise. Great for balance. Catastrophic for sperm and egg production. Again, this is something I learned too late. My infertility was 'undiagnosed' by the medical profession.

For years I tried without success to get pregnant. I tried everything apart from the IVF I was offered, as by that point I was fed-up with it all and not wanting the process. What I didn't realise at the time was two things. Firstly, my mind was saying to my body: "Are you crazy? You can barely get through your 12–hour days, fuelled by adrenalin and coffee. You don't even sleep at night due to worry and you want to grow a healthy baby in this environment? You want to time the birth so you can be back at work in 48 hours? No deal!" and because of my being the major breadwinner, my progesterone levels were no doubt sky high and my husband's depleted.

When I was running my PR company in the 90s, I learned lots of boardroom tricks to help women succeed. Women smile to please; men smile when pleased. Note to Self: don't smile like a loon. Adopt a power pose. Sit in a power position at the boardroom table (never with your back to the door). Match and mirror the power player to create rapport. Modulate your voice. The list goes on and on. On top of all of this try to be creative, professional and organised on four hours of sleep and look great. It is exhausting.

Reset! A Blueprint for a Better Life

Plus, there is the internal dialogue that runs through your mind of "I am not enough", "I just don't feel educated enough", "Someone is going to figure out that I'm flying by the seat of my pants and it will all come crashing down around me".

Ah, the imposter syndrome. I met a billionaire recently who revealed he can't enjoy his early retirement and money as he feels he did nothing incredible to gain it and that he doesn't deserve it. He is an imposter. Check out most people in boardrooms and they are probably feeling the same. Their internal dialogue is: "Behind this mask, I'm terrified. I don't really know what I'm doing. If I stay quiet and nod occasionally, maybe I can pull it off and look wise when really I am lost."

Faced with such feelings, many turn to the comfort of control and certainty. They adopt patterns of behaviour that seek to control their external environment. They start to walk a fine line between orderliness and OCD. What your subconscious mind is saying in this instance is: "I can't control that scary external world where I'm not really protected, so I can gain certainty and control at home. As long as the dishwasher has all the spoons together, forks together and knives not only together but blades facing down, then I'm in charge, all is well and I can feel OK."

So the new route out of employment for many high flyers is to move to part-time work in the same company or industry, then move to consultancy work and, if fortunate, to a well-remunerated Non-Executive director role. If they are really fortunate and have a good pension, they may choose an unpaid Non-Executive role in a NGO or similar, but what about the non-high flyers? What is their route out? Voluntary redundancy? Retirement and volunteering at the local hospice shop?

All are possible, but with the move from a company or profession one knows and is recognised for comes the opposite of the Hierarchy of Needs. This is happening increasingly to those who do not choose to leave their work but who are made redundant through changes in the workplace. Perhaps robotics will take over and make your job obsolete? Another High Street shop is boarded up because they cannot sell things as it is so easy to buy at a click from Amazon, or actually you realise that you don't need to buy at all.

Women in particular are people pleasers. They try to please everyone: their parents, boss, partner, children, friends, neighbours and co-workers. They want to be appreciated and accepted and are often conditioned to feel that only through actions will they gain love. The problem is, they forget to please themselves, and do this for so long that they don't even know what this looks or feels like. That is why some go on a journey of self-discovery after a life event such as a divorce.

Because you are reading this book, you are probably like me and into self-discovery, taking a chance, hitting the road and going on such a journey. The caveat is that many people I have met (and I have even fallen into the trap myself) never know when they have arrived. This is known as the Hedonic Treadmill. When we look for happiness and fulfilment in the future, we are depriving ourselves of it in the moment. The aims are constantly changing and you never reach the finish line.

Life is a journey and it is a journey that should be enjoyed. The journey is into yourself. It is about tapping into your true self, knowing yourself, sharing yourself through intimacy (or as the brilliant relationship expert, Ester Perel, puts it 'Into Me See'), creating a vision of the life you want to live and starting to live it now.

CHAPTER TWO

Understanding the simplicity of your complicated brain

Two monks are about to cross a river with a strong current. As the monks are preparing to cross the river, they see a very young and beautiful woman also attempting to cross. The young woman asks if they could help her cross to the other side.

The two monks glance at one another because they have taken vows not to touch a woman.

Then, without a word, the older monk picks up the woman, carries her across the river, places her gently on the other side and continues on his journey.

The younger monk can't believe what has just happened. After rejoining his companion, he is speechless and an hour passes without a word being spoken between them.

Two more hours pass, then three, and finally the younger monk can't contain himself any longer and asks angrily: "As monks, we are not permitted to touch a woman, how could you have felt able to carry that woman on your shoulders?"

The older monk looks at him with tenderness and replies, "Brother, I set her down on the other side of the river, why are you still carrying her?"

This simple Zen story illustrates a notion, known by Buddhist monks as 'Upādāna' or 'clinging' which refers to the failure to let go of what no longer serves you emotionally. This is said to be caused by 'tanhā' or 'craving, which refers to the constant desire for more, never becoming fully satisfied with what you have at this current moment.

This powerful message has helped me many times to leave hurts and burdens at the river and live in the moment as I walk up the mountain. Too often we carry around past hurts, guilt, resentment and negative emotions like bricks in a backpack, or as another saying I'm always mindful of goes: "If you don't forgive and let go it is like carrying around a cup filled with poison but the only person sipping from it is yourself". The only person we really burden and hurt is our self. It depletes us of energy, joy and ultimately our health and life itself. It is just too high a price to pay. It doesn't matter whether it is justified anger or resentment. It's not about right or wrong. If we were wronged and the other person is irredeemable, unrepentant and seemingly indifferent to our suffering, only we ourselves can stop our suffering and let it go and live a happy life again. Oh yes, I hear you say. Easier said than done.

Well, if staying stuck is easier as it is familiar and takes no effort to change, then ask yourself a question: "Am I willing to pay the price for buying this ticket". If your ticket has 'Change is too difficult so I will stay stuck' written on it, then are you willing to pay the ticket price of feeling resentful, hurt, angry and hard done by every day until you die? If your ticket says: 'The thing that happened to me was so terrible that never again

Reset! A Blueprint for a Better Life

can I have a close relationship with anyone', then that is fine if you realise that the ticket price will be a life without intimacy. Perhaps such a price is worth paying for you as your life is filled and you have connections through your career, friends, family, pets, hobbies, etc. If this is the case, then this particular ticket is worth purchasing, but if you just feel lonely and lost, are craving love and connection and all the things this brings, or you are filling up your emptiness when you get home (or even while at work) with food or drugs or possessions, then you are paying way over the odds for this choice. You really need to ask yourself: "Is this price worth paying until the day I die?" What's more, you may realise deep down that you are actually speeding up this particular journey as it is not much fun. The time to the final destination almost can't come quickly enough.

Any pain or trauma can be lived through if you are willing and able to let go. Whatever path you choose, believe with your heart and soul that you can let go and can find your joy and passion and life again. You can consciously let go of a thought pattern, hurt or behaviour if you really make up your mind to do so by understating what it is costing you to keep doing it. Sometimes the hurt is so deep that you have to let go of it, via therapy, at a subconscious level. Recognising it is the first step. Rather like letting go of a bad habit such as biting your nails for example. You determine to let the habit go as it makes your hands look awful and you keep getting sore throats from putting germ-filled fingers in your mouth repeatedly. You catch yourself bringing your hand to your mouth and consciously move it away, or perhaps you even paint your nails with foul-tasting varnish so that if you put them in your mouth you become aware of it. Eventually with repetition you let go of the habit. Letting go of hurts is the same.

Poor souls such as Amy Winehouse truly believe that they cannot be fixed by anyone or anything. They hold drinks parties in their room at rehab. It makes them feel temporarily connected, a rebel with a cause, and then in the words from the Roger Waters' song, covered by the Scissor Sisters, *Comfortably Numb*. Such a pattern can ultimately destroy them. They never learn to leave their burdens at the side of the river like the wise monk. They sip the poison from their own chalice.

To really help you in this process, you need to understand a few fundamental things about the brain. Long-term memories are actually made up of synapses or links in the brain called Neural Pathways. Some memories (called Semantic Memories) are easy to retrieve because they were more intense, as, in addition to the event itself happening, there was also a high degree of emotion or thoughts at the time which create more links to the brain and hardwire that memory into you. Sadly, this can often be based on a very traumatic rather than a very ecstatic memory.

After years of studying and paying vast sums to therapists (psychotherapy, psychology, CBT and hypnotherapy) plus a dependence on antidepressants and sleeping pills, I read a lot about the brain. I am fascinated by it and don't have anything negative to say about any of the people who have tried to help me, and how I've tried to educate or help myself and how positive things have happened. I'm not so keen to endorse the pharmaceutical route of numbing yourself via prescription drugs, non-prescription drugs or other substances. In my experience they usually backfire.

So it was a great and refreshing breakthrough for me to learn from Marisa Peer that by just knowing four fundamental things about your brain, you can really change for the better how you think, feel and behave.

Reset! A Blueprint for a Better Life

1. **Your mind does exactly what it thinks you want it to do.**

It is wired to keep you alive and do what is in your best interest, even to the extent of the man chopping off his own arm with a blunt pocket knife to survive in sub-zero temperatures after his arm became wedged in between rocks following a climbing accident. If you say: "I'm dying under this pressure, work is killing me", your mind will encourage you to survive by bunking off, making you ill or keeping you in a familiar and protective loop of procrastination. If you say: "I'm dreading that presentation. I would do anything to get out of it", your brain says: "Leave it to me!" and bingo, it gives you a migraine or panic attack. Job done. No more presentation.

2. **Your mind will always move you to pleasure and away from pain.**

The regions of the brain that are in charge of these 'fight or flight' and primeval, basic aspects are the brainstem and the cerebellum, which are often referred to as the 'reptilian' brain. We are basically doing the same things as we did when we were reptiles before mammals. The sophisticated elements of our brains that we draw on and take comfort from – attention, consciousness, perception, reasoning – all derive from a part of the brain called the neocortex. Neo means new. He was also in *The Matrix* and took an interesting pill.

Do you have a food that you just can't eat? Why? Because it made you so sick once and the memory still remains? Possibly to the point where you just believe you are allergic to it? Your brain, wired from the imprinted bad memory, wants to move you away from pain to pleasure and keeps you away from that food, as the very sight, thought or smell of it is enough to make you sick. The brain is so good at this that sadly it kicks in with other things. Things that don't work in your interest at all.

If you link pain to getting up early and exercising, then it won't happen. However much you say to yourself: "I will wake up early and run for five miles" it just doesn't happen, regularly. You just turn off the alarm and make another excuse, or your brain makes you pull a hamstring or get sick just to really help you avoid this 'pain'. You link pain to being successful perhaps? You don't realise that you do. You want to be successful and enjoy the fruits of your labour. You have invested in expensive training courses, set your business up, have lovely Moo business cards printed and then self-sabotage that same business, for example by going online for hours on trivial things.

A drug addict who is so addicted to the pleasure and release of the hard drug will inject it into their eyeball or between their toes, as that injection into their body brings pleasure and release. For someone fearful of needles, they are to be avoided or they bring pain.

Only by understanding where the pain came from originally and why your brain is still wired in a cycle of avoidance can you overcome it. Invariably, and I cite hundreds of client therapy examples here, many people find that it stems back to a series of childhood incidents. With the example of performing a presentation, perhaps you were made to stand up in class when you hated reading, possibly were dyslexic and it was not recognised, or just plain embarrassed? You had to stand there quivering and with faltering voice read a poem or difficult stanza with no respite, so you stumbled, grew embarrassed and were then humiliated by either the teacher or the other pupils or often, sadly, both. Once you sat down you closed down. That was it. No more of this pain. A second or third instance along the same lines and you have a pain that your subconscious will do all it can to help you to avoid. Fast forward to today, you love your job and want to nail this important speech. "No" your subconscious says. "We are never going there again." You try to push through. Breathing deeply to try and stem the rising panic and ease that tight and heavy feeling in your chest. "No" again. Your brain will put out more ammunition. Probably something physical like a really bad tummy upset or possibly a panic attack if you are really not paying attention.

3. **Your mind responds only to two things: the pictures in your head and the words you say (mostly to yourself).**

When you reset yourself for success, you must change these as the pictures and words will change everything. You may have heard of Pavlov and his dogs. He repeatedly rang a bell before feeding them so that they associated the bell with food. After some time, when he rang the bell the dogs had a physical response and created saliva in their mouths even if no food was present or given. Why do men going to give a sperm sample get given a copy of a girly magazine? They don't go into that small cubicle with actual women, it is their imagination and visualising these sexy women that does the trick.

Your brain doesn't care if what you tell it is good or bad, right or wrong, real or imagined. Stress creates physical symptoms in the body. I've had a few severe panic attacks and believe me, you think you are actually dying. The physical symptoms are intense, including profound sweating, vomiting, diarrhoea and nearly blacking out. Go for a physical checkup after such an incident and you will get the all clear.

© Marisa Peer Rules of Your Mind

Close your eyes just for one minute, and imagine that in your right hand you have a huge half-cut juicy lemon. The kind you can pick straight off a tree in Italy or Spain that has thick white pith inside and is literally bursting with juice and freshness. Lift the lemon up under your nose (with your eyes still shut) and breathe in that zingy vibrant aroma. It is so fresh. That is why so many cleaning products are lemon scented. It feels like life and freshness. Now open your mouth and still totally visualising that lemon in your hand squeeze it and let the juice trickle into your mouth. Feel your tongue come alive as the sharp and acid juice hits it. Swill it around your mouth and wake up every taste bud. Then swallow. Open your eyes. There was really no lemon but your brain didn't care. The visualisation and sensory experience was just as real as reality itself.

That's why certain situations will be pleasurable or exciting for many and terrifying for others. Take high altitude skiing or extreme sports for example. To the risk takers, the idea of dropping out of a helicopter into virgin snow and skiing off-piste is as good as it gets. To others, who are afraid of heights or think that skiing in potentially life-threatening conditions is madness, it is not. If you have ever been afraid of flying or flown with someone who is, you will be aware of the fear and panic that sets in, often weeks before the flight. Such people will do all their washing and wear matching underwear as they go over and over again a visualisation of crashing, of a 'flying coffin', and of them being laid out ready for identification. To everyone else, even though flying is now more arduous with all the necessary safety checks, thoughts instead turn to what they will be doing soon after arrival. Whatever it is and wherever they are going, it will be a positive visualisation. Their images that their brain latches onto are good ones. They feel good. It is the same event: a flight, but people are making different words and pictures to associate with it and the brain is taking these as true, so people are having very different responses.

One of the major causes of depression is the harsh critical words we say to ourselves and not knowing or feeling or believing that "I Am Enough". Marisa Peer has reached millions of people with this simple yet profound message via her talks and courses. Scientists know that self-praise is the most effective. Sometimes external praise can come with a hidden agenda as your boss leans in and tells you what an utterly invaluable part of the team you are just before asking you to work all weekend. The praise you give yourself has no such catch.

I run workshops. I always guide people through this exercise and I am always met with resistance from many of my clients. I ask: "Can everyone close their eyes? Now say out loud 'I am...' and add a positive word to the end of the phrase such as 'I am smart', 'I am lovable', 'I am attractive'". I urge them to keep adding words and saying the phrase and say what they believe. This is often the part where it grinds to a bit of a halt. People who are used to saying to themselves on a daily basis "I am such an idiot" or "I am such a waste of space" or "I am incapable of being loved or finding the one" can barely get past "I am nice" or "I am kind to animals". So I ask them to add what they want to hear, such as "I am beautiful inside and out" or "I am intelligent". In the end, I get them to settle for "I am enough", not because I feel it is weaker than something such as "I am amazing". No, it is because it is really the crux of all our self-doubt and self-loathing. Just not feeling we are enough. That's why the rich and famous who look like they have everything can lead miserable lives or end up dying young if they don't believe this about themselves.

So you need to own the phrase and reinforce it daily. You can get lovely bracelets with it engraved on them. A friend of mine has it tattooed on her wrist. I have it written on my dressing table mirror in lipstick. In fact, when I had a new cleaner a few years ago and asked her never to wipe it off, a conversation about what those words meant ensued and she referred her self-harming daughter to me for therapy, and then her husband saw me for an issue we worked together to resolve.

Another phrase that can reset you is 'choosing'. So instead of groaning when it is a sunny Sunday and you have a report to write that you have put off doing all weekend, say out loud: "My business will ultimately give me freedom. I am choosing to do whatever it takes to make my business a success and I feel good about that". This simple mind hack can change your life. Your brain will get on board. The resistance will diminish and you will not only get the task done quickly, remain in a better frame of mind and thus maintain a better ease of body, but you will also feel great about yourself afterwards. It may even help to set up a reward. Report completed in three hours = two hours at the pool, gym, or movies. Whatever works for you.

4. Your mind loves what is familiar and dislikes the unfamiliar.

This pattern plays out across the world every day. The Premier League football player who compromises his career because he can't face that move to AC Milan with his wife?

© Marisa Peer Rules of Your Mind

38   Reset! A Blueprint for a Better Life

The lottery winner who spends it all, because that is their familiar pattern each weekend on getting a wage on a Friday?

Yet challenge the 'familiar' or the known or the believed in, and it can tumble like a house of cards. For thousands of years people believed that the human body was not capable of running a mile in less than four minutes. Yet a man called Roger Bannister decided he would do just that. In addition to his gruelling physical training, he visualised every day the achievement in order to create a sense of certainty in his mind and body. On 6 May 1954, under monitored conditions, he ran a mile in 3 minutes 59.4 seconds. Less than a year after he did this, his record was smashed and continues to be. Today it is almost routine, even athletic high school boys can run a mile in under four minutes

When you become certain of something, focus on it intently every day then something amazing happens, and it is not magic, it is science. We have a system in our bodies called the reticular activating system (RAS) that is the portal through which nearly all information enters the brain. It helps our brains to decide what information to focus on and what to delete. At its most basic, the RAS will respond to your name, anything that is a threat and information that is needed immediately. It also responds to novelty: looks for the new so that you notice something different, out of place. It draws your attention. As it is wired in this way, understanding it and working with it means you can also rewire or reset yourself for success.

Your mind is also wired for some stress, which was initially a survival mechanism as it kicks you into fight or flight mode when backed into a corner by a sabre-toothed-tiger. It can still be good in small doses, but many CEOs, athletes and top performers have the mistaken belief that it is their stress that gives them an edge. It may drive them and get them through many situations, but eventually it will elicit a very hefty price and this is actually happening on a daily basis as they, and you, stress your body and cloud your mind.

When you experience stress, your body releases a series of chemical reactions. It floods your body with acid designed to shut down your digestive system to free you up to run immediately. It also seeps into your skin to make you not taste so good (perhaps Mr Tiger won't like your flavour), your blood will coagulate to save you from bleeding to death if bitten, and your bladder and bowels will evacuate, again to lighten you up for faster flight. Your vision will narrow down to focus on your adversary and an escape route. Stress floods your body with adrenaline, noradrenaline and cortisol, but stress in our lives is now flooding the body on a daily basis with these acids and is very damaging to your health. It can lead to excess belly fat, erectile dysfunction, infertility, premature ageing and premature atrophy of the brain.

Also, when in this mode with your body flooded with acid, your immune system takes a back seat. Who cares about a long-term or future disease if you are about to be eaten? Your mind has your back. It will prioritise for you, but the mismatch now, when you are facing yet another gruelling business meeting rather than another wild animal, causes dis-ease in your mind and body and spirit. It will dis-allow you to perform at the top of your game as you are reacting physically and emotionally to something one of your ancestors clearly avoided thousands of years ago to allow all that DNA to go down the generations until you were born.

These primeval patterns of thinking that we are hardwired with also lead to a plethora of unwanted behaviours and feelings. There is so much neuroscience to back this up now and to point the way forward to heathier ways of thinking and thus being that you can't discount it. You may not choose to do anything about it but the evidence is now there.

If you can't control the inner turmoil in your mind and body (often identified by that knot or sinking feeling in your stomach, perhaps accompanied by sleepless nights and IBS or constant digestive issues), where will it lead? Disease or to be precise dis-ease. While I am not a big supporter of the 'you created your own cancer' school of thought as I don't find a hefty dose of guilt or self-loathing helps recovery, I do see that our thoughts and behaviours can definitely create the 'soil' or conditions in which dis-ease can take a hold and grow, or they can block something we think we want.

I tried in vain for years to get pregnant. I didn't present myself for testing until we had been trying for two years as I didn't want to 'talk myself into having a problem'. Then a barrage of intrusive tests ensued. Sex became automated to fit in with my monthly cycle and most fertile periods. I turned to every available complementary therapy I could find including Ayurvedic medicine, kinesiology, spiritual cleansing, acupuncture, floatation tanks, past life regression, massage, high-protein diets, low-protein diets, supplements and magnetic therapy.

Ayurvedic medicine (also called Ayurveda) originated in India more than 3,000 years ago and remains one of the country's traditional health care systems. It diagnoses the whole body not just the dis-ease and aims to rebalance the body through herbal compounds, special diets, and other unique health practices such as acupuncture. If you want an Ayurvedic doctor, then areas where there is a large Indian population such as in parts of Leicester offer a wide selection. Kinesiology is a hybrid of Chiropractic muscle testing techniques and Chinese Medicine with elements of Ayurvedic Medicine and Counselling added in. It focuses on body, mind and spirit and the connections between the physical body, emotional and biochemical stress.

A session takes place on a treatment table and the practitioner uses acupressure points to test for imbalances in the muscle system of the body. I found it helped me to release a lot of stored-up tension and I actually had a very spiritual experience whilst the treatment was happening, sensing many people in the room who I felt were relatives or guides standing watch over me in a healing sort of way. This is the first time I've shared that experience of more than 20 years ago.

A trained spiritual healer can discern disturbance and imbalances in the person's aura and chakras. Spiritual cleansing is about replacing negative or otherwise undesirable energy with positive, desirable energy. It can be done remotely and often it is to do with your surroundings – my house was very compromised for some time (both in London and the Bahamas) due to bad energies that came in.

Floatation tanks were very trendy in the 90s. My husband and I went for a weekend to a retreat that specialised in them. Flotation Therapy is essentially a way of achieving deep relaxation by spending an hour or more lying quietly in darkness, suspended in a warm solution of Epsom salts. Float tanks are also known as isolation tanks, sensory deprivation tanks and REST (Restricted Environmental Stimulation Therapy) chambers. It was an odd experience. I didn't mind the enclosed space, finding it rather womb like and I liked floating in the salty warm water with soothing music playing all around. However, I didn't really feel anything much and became rather bored. Returning to our hotel room I said to my husband that it was pleasant but I did not see what it had really achieved. I then sat down on the floor by the bed and burst into tears and sobbed for about an hour. Whatever it released I found it very cathartic, and slept for hours afterwards.

Magnetic therapy is based on the understanding that our bodies have an electro-magnetic field (iron makes up about 4% of our blood and every cell in our body produces an electrical impulse), so magnets can reset or heal this field if it is compromised or dis-eased. I had read that many pet beds contain magnets and can heal animals of many complaints. This was compelling to me because you can discount the placebo effect for an animal as it simply doesn't know about it.

After this rather exhausting search for a 'cure' at the time of trying to conceive, my husband's tests came back as normal. I was then diagnosed with Unspecific Infertility. What I failed to realise at the time was that it was my mind that was the block and it was stopping any pregnancy in a compromised body with a rather ambiguous attitude towards the whole idea of motherhood.

If disease isn't manifesting for you (yet), then you may be adopting a blocking strategy like I was to subconsciously move you away from pain or block it out in a temporary way.

Fired from your job for poor performance? Let's block it out by drinking to oblivion becomes the subconscious reaction. I knew a man who sadly drank himself to death. He went bankrupt in the 90s. On his way back from the bankruptcy hearing, he purchased a car. This was the final straw for his wife who had stood by him up to this point even though they had lost their house and business and had put huge strain on the children. When I asked him why on earth he did it (on falsified credit, so the car soon went back), he said he wanted to feel like he used to feel (the familiar) and again feel that he was really a success. The car was a status symbol or a mask.

Distorted self-image is one of the biggest issues I help to deal with in my therapeutic practice. As already mentioned, the additional social media pressures of putting your best face ('edited' me) forward is crippling the young in particular, with anxiety and creating a loss of individuality. This is what happens to so many people, especially high-performing business people. They wear the mask. They feel like imposters. Even the ones the rest of us emulate. Actor Kate Winslet said: "Sometimes I wake up in the mornings before going off to a shoot and I think, I can't do this. I'm a fraud." The disconnect between this external self (ego) and their true inner self gets wider and wider and the pain gets deeper. We are scared and scarred inside.

"Ah, so if my inner self is so much in turmoil, then perhaps by controlling my external world I will feel better." This is the path to Obsessive Compulsive Disorder (or OCD) tendencies, or we control ourselves and our bodies in unhealthy ways such as by bulimia. I was bulimic for a year and no one noticed. I had had Dengue Fever and lost 26lbs, going from a UK size 12 to a size 4. This was the era of the size 00 model. Thin was in. I was delighted. Weighing in at just under 7 stone (95 lbs.) I had the body of my dreams, or that is what I saw in the mirror at the time. Now I see a painfully thin woman with rather gaunt cheeks and no breasts. However, when I recovered from the illness, the lifestyle I was conducting while still running my London PR company meant the pounds started to creep on. I'd read that Princess Diana was bulimic and I decided at some level (conscious or subconscious) that I could still go to all the client and journalist breakfasts, lunches and dinners and stay at my new perfect weight with the help of regular trips to the toilet and a toothbrush carried in my handbag. Luckily, I broke the pattern myself as I could no longer lie to myself that this was healthy for my body, but I understand why it happened and have compassion for the me at that time that embraced it as a solution.

Another mask is anger. Anger is a secondary emotion that is there to mask or protect the true emotion behind it, which is usually hurt. For many years, anger was my go-to emotion. I became really good at it. An extensive vocabulary allowed barbed words to be delivered for maximum impact. When that wasn't enough I had a period of breaking things. Thankfully this didn't last long, but Villeroy & Boch did well out of me as I replaced glasses that had been thrown to the floor in the heat of my anger. I hated myself for it. I didn't realise that I was just incredibly hurt and hurting. That my ability to cope with all that was expected of me, demanded of me, required of me was not enough.

The next time you find yourself getting angry, take a moment, sit and take three deep breaths, breathing into your stomach first, with your tongue on the roof of your mouth, and exhaling slowly through your mouth as if blowing out candles and say: "I am hurting now. X has hurt me (a person, an event, etc.) and I am very hurt and this hurt will pass. I choose to let it pass and I do not choose anger or feeling bad during the process." Then do the breaths again. Realise that you are quite a simple being in your responses and patterns of behaviour and don't dismiss this simple solution.

When we find ourselves empty, we fill ourselves up in different ways. Shopping. Alcohol. Exercise. Work. Sex. Food. The ways are endless. I was once told that I had an addictive personality. Possibly true, but also not entirely helpful. I moved my addiction and ways of being filled up around all of those unhealthy choices, plus several more for good measure.

And over and over again we just stay stuck. Like the story of the whining dog on the nail, we don't have enough pain to galvanise us to change. If you are not familiar with the story, the potted version is this: On a street with porches and pooches a man notices that every day as he walks to work all the dogs bar one bark at him. One just sits and whimpers and moans as if he is in pain. This happens every day for a week until the man, unable to walk past this dog and ignore its discomfort, knocks on the door of the house and when the owner answers, asks him why his dog is whining and moaning. The owner replies: "It's because he is sitting on a nail." The man is surprised and says: "What?! Your dog is sitting on a nail. Why doesn't he get off?" "Well, it just doesn't hurt him enough," comes the reply.

We stay stuck because it just doesn't hurt enough. Yet.

We fear the change or transition into the unfamiliar. As Shakespeare says: *Our doubts are traitors and make us lose the ground we oft might win by fearing the attempt.* The biggest challenge to this perfectly sensible piece of motivational wisdom is our mind. Specifically, our repeating stories. The monkey on our shoulder or whatever term you choose to give it. This can range from the simple inner critical voice of: "Who are you to think you can do this?" to "You will just screw this up like you ruin everything" right through to the really embedded: "I can never be happy/successful because of the damage inflicted on me in my childhood. My father beat my ambition out of me. My mother told me I'd never amount to anything. All our family are losers. I'll never get over this conditioning. It's just who I am."

Empathy is one of my strong points. I delight in transitioning people from lives of pain to lives of joy and fulfilment, but patterns of thought such as this have to be eradicated. The past is a concept (as is the future). It was real at some point, but when you get stuck in a story you just keep investing in it and making what is really a concept, or half-remembered event, real. The only person this is now real for is you.

Traumatic events are never desired, but when they do happen, how your life will be after the event is all down to how you are able to view or process that event. This may take some heavy lifting, and again there is a range of wonderful therapies and other forms of help available, but don't get stuck reliving the event for years and years. Find a transformational therapy that will let you make sense of the trauma and let it go as quickly as possible.

For me, the traumatic imprint of being attacked in a multi-storey car park one sunny afternoon in central Nottingham in 1985 was not one that was forgotten easily.

The man sprang out as I exited my car and tried to abduct me by pushing me into the passenger seat foot well, shouting at me and starting the car. Quick thinking allowed me to distract him by saying that my boyfriend (I was alone) was at the driver's window and when he turned around to look, I reached over, grabbed the key from the ignition and stuck it in his eye and pushed him half out of the still open door. He pulled me with him by my hair and a struggle ensued. I had only one thought: "I'm not going with you!" He threw me on the car park floor. I had one more thought: "You have now ruined my new dress, you bastard!" I fought like a wildcat and I escaped.

When I saw the photofit of his face in *The Sun* 14 years after the attack, my blood ran cold. There he was. Scotland Yard confirmed I was one of the few of his victims who got away to tell the tale. I had been able to recall after all that time such details that they knew it was him without a doubt. He was the UK's most prolific serial rapist who abducted his victims and had become increasingly violent towards them.

The important lesson is this. I found it empowering that I had got away. We all wonder how we will react in a time of danger and challenge and I found out that I don't play victim. It gave me comfort. I didn't exactly go wandering the streets in the small hours of the morning with some naïve belief that I was invincible, but it brought me through many further times of challenge, the breast cancer for one.

Whether you think you can or you can't, you are right. This is why Sports Psychology is such an important and profitable business. Just watch Wimbledon or the Olympics and you will hear repeatedly the commentators saying: "Their biggest battle in this past season has been with themselves". In a world such as the men's 100m Olympic race where the 1st, 2nd and 3rd placeholders are separated by tiny fractions of a second and their human bodies are trained to the peak of their performance, the difference is the mind.

Muhammad Ali said and believed "I am the greatest". He would also visualise and focus on the exact outcome of his fights. In a famous 15 November 1962 photo, young heavyweight boxer (then named) Cassius Clay points to a sign he wrote on a chalk board in his dressing room before

Reset! A Blueprint for a Better Life

his fight against Archie Moore in Los Angeles, predicting he'd knock Moore out in the fourth round, which he went on to do. The sign also predicts Clay will be the next champ via a knockout over Sonny Liston in eight rounds. He did it in seven rounds. Then named Muhammad Ali, he is seen in another photo in London on 19 June 1963 holding up eight fingers as he predicts the number of rounds it will take him to knock out Sonny Liston if he should get a chance at the world heavyweight championship. The day before, having predicted an end to his fight with British heavyweight champion Henry Cooper in five rounds at London's Wembley stadium, Ali had won on a technical knockout in the fifth round. He said later: "Not only am I the greatest, I'm the double greatest. Not only do I knock them out, I pick the round."

The U.S. Navy's research arm has developed a training program to help Marines weaponise their intuitions – in essence, pushing young riflemen to trust their guts in order to detect ambushes, spot buried bombs and know who to trust on chaotic, urban battlefields.

According to The Daily Beast that obtained details of The Office of Naval Research's four-year, $4 million 'sense-making' initiative, launched in 2014, via the Freedom of Information Act: "It's almost, but not quite, a military effort to teach Extra-Sensory Perception, or ESP".

"This is an attempt to improve what regular people already have," John Alexander, the author of *The Warrior's Edge* and an expert in fringe military research, adds. A 23-page sense-making training manual breaks it down into two distinct skills: 'perspective-taking' – basically empathy – and 'characterising', or imagination.

Clearly the military knows that perception or mindfulness, just as in sport, can make the difference between winning and losing. Only in this case it is about life and death.

How else can you break some of these patterns yourself?

I've attended several workshops with Sonia Choquette who is an author, spiritual teacher, six-sensory consultant and transformational visionary guide. She teaches how to tap into your inner intuitive knowing and to open your heart and listen to your heart and intuition.

Many of her exercises are meditative and she says of this that: "Meditation is not another thing to do. It's an invitation to stop doing".

She has a practice called 'I am Calm'. Try it out and do it regularly as it develops the intuitive muscle. Whenever you need a break or a moment to just be a human being rather than a human doing, simply touch your thumb and forefinger together, take a deep breath and say quietly to yourself: "I am...." as you inhale and " ... calm" as you exhale. Allow the feeling of 'calm' to reverberate throughout your entire body. The act of touching thumb to forefinger will serve as a physical reminder to come back to the moment and the words "I am calm" will wash away the stress.

As Sonia points out: "Quieting your nervous system and nurturing yourself can save you hours of wasted anxiety, sudden blowups, potential confrontations, health stress and costly oversights. It's tonic for the spirit."

Sonia also has an exercise called 'I Wonder' where you just repeatedly ask the question 'I wonder', adding different things that would serve you at that moment to the end such as: "I wonder where I'll find that parking space?" or "I wonder what my best talents are?" or "I wonder who is calling" (when your phone rings). This allows you to fill your life with wonder and be open to possibilities rather than irritated by the interruption of your phone ringing or frustrated and tense as you look for a parking spot.

It reminds me of a great mind hack I learned from Tony Robbins in the mid-90s. He taught me to ask, "What else could this mean?", just at the point when you are about to get hurt and get angry, jumping to a conclusion. The next time a shop assistant is rude to you, ask yourself, "I wonder what else this could mean?" and your clever subconscious will come up with some possibilities. Perhaps his partner shouted at him earlier?

Perhaps his boss has just given him a censure? Perhaps he is worried as his son is sick? This stops the 'drama' being about you and adds in a feeling of possibility and compassion.

I have a Gratitude Journal. This is another brilliant way to focus yourself daily on what is good. Even on the worst of days I can find something, such as: "I am grateful that as I sipped my coffee today a robin settled in the tree and made me think of my dear departed Mum". Try this one too: get a large empty jar on 1st January each year and every time something special, wonderful or touching happens, scribble it down on a piece of paper and drop it in the jar. As you approach the end of that year, perhaps in that dip between the end of Christmas and the impending New Year, take out the jar and read all the slips of paper.

Follow this link to YouTube to see about some famous failures: **https://youtu.be/zLYECIjmnQs**

Want intimacy or INTO ME SEE?
Be vulnerable. Live your truth

Many people go through life living a lie, pretending to be someone they are not and they are miserable. Live your truth. You only have one life to live. Live it your way. If family or friends do not approve, that is their problem. Do not make it yours. Clearly this is not a get-out-of-jail-free card for being completely insensitive. It is not saying, do what you want to do or say what you want to say to anyone, anytime, but it is about you allowing yourself to be your authentic and best self.

What people think of you is none of your business. Remember: "To thine own self be true." Being yourself unblocks your energy. It frees you up. It allows you to live from your power. The world is waiting for you. It is time to be you. You can't be anyone else, they are already taken.

When I cleared out the attic in my parents' home after the sad death of my father, I found boxes of items I barely remembered. My Brownie and Guide badges, rusty key rings and trinkets in a battered biscuit tin. Valentine's cards (many in my mother's handwriting that I had failed to recognise as a child!), padded birthday cards with kittens on them. Teenage love and my Twinkle Album 1968. In the front was a template saying: 'When I grow up I want to be.......' I had filled in 'An actress and a doctor in my spare time'. At that age, nothing holds us back. Want to be a spaceship captain? Why certainly. Want to be an actress and also a doctor? Why not? Walt Disney looked across an expanse of arid land in LA and didn't see orange trees. He saw Disneyland in his imagination. Now within Disney are people with job titles such as Chief Visioneer. First, you have to dream it or vision it then it becomes real.

When you are a child, before enough people (including teachers and members of one's family) have said: "Don't be silly, you can't do that..." or, in the case of a recent client of mine, "You are not cut out for the BIG stuff, just lower your expectations", you had dreams. The big challenge is that after others stop saying "no" or "don't be silly" to us, we are so hardwired that we continue the dialogue with ourselves, every single day. "Who am I to think I can get that job/partner/lifestyle?" Better not to try than face the hurt and humiliation of failure.

In psychology, this concept is known as the Internal Corrections Officer. When you are young, your parents, teachers, etc, take on the role of the 'corrections officer', telling you "don't be silly" or "lower your expectations". When you are older, you internalise this and in the absence of those adults you become your own corrections officer, telling yourself that you are no good.

Ask yourself today: "What would I dare to dream if nothing is in the way?" As you imagine, be careful to make it a 'How' free zone. In business and life, you need those who focus on the 'how'. It's important but it can also stifle dreams.

I'm a 'What' person. 'What if we could... what would this look like?' A visioneer. Clearly you need a team to support your vision, including the 'How' people. Otherwise you may decide to get to the other side of the river but have no idea how to build the bridge, or you start to build the bridge with no idea of how it will be secured at the other side. Focusing on 'How' in this scenario will mean that you are left standing on the bank of the river waiting for a ferryman. 'How' will never move you forward with a vision or life purpose if you get caught up on it.

So back to the question: what would you dare to dream if nothing was in the way? A different job? House? Lifestyle? Body? Relationship? Let's face it, if Donald Trump can imagine being President of the USA and pull it off, anything is possible!

Take a moment now. Grab a pen and paper or just close your eyes and visualise. What would you dream? If everything were available to you and everything were possible, what would your life and body and inner self look and feel like?

Then ask yourself: What made you happy at eight years old? If you imagine yourself to be eight sitting in front of the Twinkle Album, question what might you have written. Then think further. In between the ages of 8 and 17, before you had to be channelled into a job, or career, or university degree or next life stage, what did you dream of?

Often what made us happy as children reveals our true self. At age eight I loved to read and write. I wrote poems and short stories and won prizes for them. Suffering ill health often, I would be at home and with no daytime TV or computers or apps the option was to read and write. My imagination knew no bounds. I found it hard to fall asleep as I was convinced all my toys came alive at night and once, just once, I wanted to see it for myself. Sadly I never did, but those toys are tricksy, don't you know?!

The Power of the Law of Attraction

I love Vision Boards (also called Mood Boards). Start by surrounding yourself with piles of amassed magazines and brochures and cut out the things you would like to see in this ideal vision of your life. Then stick them all to one giant board. The process is fun, but the reason I love them is because they create massive focus in you. As you look at the completed board every day, at a subliminal level you start to move towards those goals. You see them as if they are already part of your life. Your mind sees these visions as real, as it can't tell the difference between what is and what is imagined. That is why worry is so insidious. You make pictures in your mind and your mind thinks they are real and so it has a stress response.

Something greater happens too. At a metaphysical level, you start to manifest those goals. This is a concept that may seem rather 'woo woo' to some, but watch the movie (or read the book) *The Secret* and decide at the end of it if you now think it so strange, as one intelligent, articulate, successful person after person shares stories of how they recovered financially or health wise by having a singular vision of what their life would look like.

Quite simply, the book and movie state that your thoughts control the universe. Through this law of attraction, you manifest your desires, like placing an order from a catalogue. You have to be specific. You must know that what you want is yours the moment you ask, so for example if you see yourself living in abundance you will attract it.

The author Rhonda Byrne says this: "Be grateful for what you have now. As you begin to think about all the things in your life you are grateful for, you will be amazed at the never ending thoughts that come back to you of more things to be grateful for. You have to make a start and then the law of attraction will receive those grateful thoughts and give you more just like them."

Says contributor John Assaraf: "You become what you think about most, but you also attract what you think about most." This is reinforced by Bob Proctor who adds: "You will attract everything that you require. If it's money you need, you will attract it. If it's people you need, you'll attract it. You've got to pay attention to what you're attracted to, because as you hold images of what you want, you're going to be attracted to things and they're going to be attracted to you, but it literally moves into physical reality with and through you and it does that by law."

"A lot of people feel like they're victims in life and they'll often point to past events, perhaps growing up with an abusive parent or in a dysfunctional family. Most psychologists believe that about 85% of families are dysfunctional, so all of a sudden you're not so unique. My parents were alcoholics. My dad abused me. My mother divorced him when I was six... I mean, that's almost everybody's story in some form or not. The real question is, what are you going to do now? What do you choose now? Because you can either keep focusing on that, or you can focus on what you want, and when people start focusing on what they want, what they don't want falls away and what they want expands and the other part disappears." – Jack Canfield

One major contributor is Lisa Nichols, who I've had the pleasure of meeting several times at A-Fest and working with on one of her excellent Mastermind Days. She warns that: "When you focus on lack and scarcity and what you don't have, you fuss about it with your family, you discuss it with your friends, you tell your children that you don't have enough – 'We don't have enough for that, we can't afford that' – then you'll never be able to afford it, because you begin to attract more of what you don't have. If you want abundance, if you want prosperity, then focus on abundance. Focus on prosperity."

The final words from *The Secret* go to Marci Shimoff, with the salutary advice that: "Many people in Western culture are striving for success. They want the great home, they want their business to work, they want all these outer things, but what we found in our research is that having these outer things does not necessarily guarantee what we really want, which is happiness. So we go for these outer things thinking they're going to bring us happiness, but it's backward. You need to go for the inner joy, the inner peace, the inner vision first and then all of the outer things appear."

At a book festival I went to hear the story of champion jockey Declan Murphy who had finally allowed journalist Ami Rao to write the story of his career, near fatal accident and return to not only health but championship status. I was totally blown away. Declan's honesty and openness were breathtaking. He spoke openly of how his survival and life now was entirely due to determination and belief. These qualities, plus a great deal of synchronicity and something akin to divine intervention, helped him to defy the odds and survive, but for many years this was merely a physical survival. Only when he worked with Ami and was vulnerable enough to tell his story did he truly

Reset! A Blueprint for a Better Life

live again. The resulting book *Centaur – The memoir of the jockey who came back from the dead* is a beautiful story. A read. A ride. A revelation. As Declan says: "Nobody sees the fight within you. They see what they see with their eyes; they don't see your spirit. On the outside I looked fine and nobody knew what was happening on the inside. No one knew the truth. This book is my truth."

In case you are not familiar with it, synchronicity is a sort of alignment of events, people or things that seem beyond something random. The psychotherapist Carl Jung created the term after he experienced 'meaningful coincidences' where two or more signs that occurred randomly were also connected by meaning (not by cause) in both his life and during sessions with clients. For example, back in my PR days I once really needed to get hold of a client who was avoiding my calls. It was literally keeping me awake at night, and a few days later in London I had to catch the tube that I normally avoided at all costs. Sitting in the carriage there he was, smack bang opposite me. I'm not sure who was most surprised, he or I. However, the difficult conversation we needed to have then took place.

So how do you even find your truth? Most people, when asked what they want in life, just can't answer. I come across this daily. My clients submit an intake form and tell me of the issues they wish to deal with and be rid of. Part of my form asks the question: "If this condition could be removed, how would you like to feel/behave?" Usually people will fill in the former questions at great length, sometimes with pages of supporting evidence for why they feel or act this way, the events that triggered it, what it costs them, etc. This is great to enable me to help them, but the section about how they want to feel is usually answered in a few lines. Invariably, the answer comes down to "I want to feel free", "I want to be able to feel joy and connection and love", "I want to know who I am and what my life purpose is", or "I want to be happy".

There are lots of ways of finding out your values and visions. There are courses that are not worth the money they charge and there are courses that are breathtakingly expensive but life-changing. Perhaps some of this is due to the fact that if you make such a huge financial investment in finding these things out, you really turn up determined to do so. This was the case when I attended the LifeBook seminar in Barcelona. I was not feeling well, having overdone the 'work hard and party hard' mantra of A-Fest in Ibiza just before it, plus spending a week with friends in Madrid, returning to the UK, seeing a month's worth of clients in a week and then immediately flying to Barcelona. Having made a large financial investment, I forced myself to go. Internally I was facing a huge dilemma. My inner critic was on a non-stop loop that took every ounce of my ability to hypnotise into submission. "You are just a course junkie!" "What will one more course bring you to realise that 20 years of personal development and life events haven't so far?" "Stop spending time and money on courses. Go earn some." That inner voice didn't ease up.

Yet I did turn up to the course. I decided to be open and vulnerable to the process. Having a chest infection and feeling rather ill actually helped. It meant I had to park my ego and just be. It meant that I couldn't reach into the old rucksack marked 'Sparkling and witty PR person mask' and put that on to hide behind. I thought: "If I can get through the day, stay open to the process and dig deep, then that is a win."

This is exactly what I did. I was aware enough of the false masks we wear. So many of us don't feel like we are our authentic selves. So many of us have to put on a mask on a daily basis to play the roles we have been cast in and yet, usually we can't remember ever auditioning for that role. Sasha Fierce vs Beyoncé. The CEO of a successful company knows how to get 'suited and booted' and to turn up to work wearing that mask and play that role, but who are they when it is 5am on a Sunday morning? If they are well balanced, they will be able to tap into their true self when not in the work environment. To play with Lego with their son or pretend to be a horse while cantering around the back garden with their daughter. Sadly, many people simply can't switch off. I decided to sell my PR company when I came home exhausted one Friday evening, another 80-hour week nearly over (I always worked at weekends too) and went to my seven-year-old son's bedroom. He was asleep and as I sat on the bed to watch him I realised I had not seen him awake since Monday morning at breakfast. Five days earlier. That was my 'Ah ha' moment. Enough.

And LifeBook had a massive 'Ah ha' moment in store for me. What I really like about LifeBook is that it is structured and yet you fill in your own content. It guides you to really dive deep inside yourself, examine your beliefs and values and then create visions that go way beyond them. On a practical level, you then have to create goals (like SMART – Specific, Measurable, Agreed upon, Realistic, Time-based) that give you a blueprint for how to actually achieve these visions. It is a sort of vision board with a to-do list. There is also a 'Stop Doing' list. What will you have to stop doing to get what you want and desire? You want a great body? Well then, stop laying on the sofa eating crisps and get outside at least for a walk. Get a

Fitbit and do a minimum of 10,000 steps a day. You want a new relationship? Well stop being stuck in one that doesn't work for you, or do some serious work and open communication within that relationship in order to fix it.

The 'Stop Doing' list was a revelation for me. I had apps on my phone and computer to create really smart to-do lists. I could even prioritise the lists by the most important goals or actions and assign timeframes to them all. I even have a great goal-setting product now (Goalsetting.training).

At that time, I forgot to stop doing things. If you want to write a book, you have to stop doing a lot of things. Reading other books for a start, unless it is for light relief at night. TV. Too much social media. Each person's list will be personal to them, but many of the time-wasting diversions we turn to will be common to all. Procrastination is the great universal. I read a great book about creative writing called *The War of Art* and remember how, when faced with having to just sit down and write, the author instead rearranges his sock drawer by colour.

My LifeBook revelation was that I had to stop trying to 'Recover' my life. I had been in recovery mode for 13 years. Recovering my health after the cancer. Recovering my sense of self and self-worth after two divorces and several moves. Recovering financially after monetary losses.

Many of my clients want to stop procrastinating. They feel like their life is always on hold. That they will never get what they want (once they know what that is).

Procrastination is fear-based. It is due to a fear of failure or not being perfect, yet perfection is unattainable. Like a finish line that is held on each side by a post on wheels. As you run and run and get closer and closer, they just keep pushing that line further away from you. You will never reach it. The effort is exhausting. Futile. Unfair. This is called the Hedonic Treadmill.

Our deepest fear as human beings is a fear of rejection. A fear of being so different that we are exiled, sent away, marooned, put into solitary confinement. All of these punishments are about separation and rejection.

People want to be connected and to belong. When Nancy Reagan launched the ill-conceived campaign against drugs in the USA in the 80s with the slogan 'Just Say No!', it was doomed to fail. The reason people say yes to being part of a gang, or yes to staying in an abusive relationship, or yes to drugs is to gain connection and avoid rejection.

It is also about worthiness. Many people feel 'I am not worthy. I am not enough'.

If you are in a relationship that sucks the life out of you, every nerve inside you is screaming that this is not right, but if you don't feel worthy enough to feel you deserve better then you will stay stuck. The intuitive part of you will either be switched off from thinking that what you want is available (like the whining dog, this is a safer place to stay), or it may be screaming out for change but doesn't know how to get there. So you don't speak up and stand up for yourself, or as Marianne Williamson said in a famous quote (that is often misattributed to Nelson Mandela): "Our deepest fear is not that we are weak. Our deepest fear is that we are powerful beyond measure. It is our light, not our darkness that most frightens us. We ask ourselves, who am I to be brilliant, gorgeous, talented, fabulous? Actually, who are you not to be? You are a child of God. Your playing small does not serve the world... As we are liberated from our own fear, our presence automatically liberates others."

Instead of tapping into our light and power, we concede to others in the mistaken belief that it will make them and us happy. This is never more painful than in love relationships (for heterosexual couples or a same-sex couple where one partner is more masculine) that are not working. Because of the inherent 'Mars' versus 'Venus' nature of men and women, when relationships, whatever stage they are at, start to unravel or be uneven, women have a tendency to seek reassurance or affirmation that they are enough. They start to try harder and harder and harder to please. If this fails and they are met with a cold lack of response, they start to ask 'why?' or 'what is the matter?' and want to resolve the perceived problem via questioning his or her feelings or asking where the relationship is going, or just by talking, talking, talking. It is a shame, as good and open and honest communication is the bedrock of an outstanding relationship, but when the man is off to his cave, trying to club him over the head with words or emotional blackmail and drag him out by his hair never works.

What can be even more difficult than letting a man go to his cave (and vice versa letting a woman talk it out) is getting to the realisation that this relationship is broken, dysfunctional, unhealthy and just won't work. From painful personal experience, I have found that once a man has decided to check out (for whatever reasons, many of which may be his fear of intimacy issues or a myriad of others), he does just that. He has made a decision and the word decide comes from the Latin word 'decido' and means 'to cut off', so that is exactly what he does. Perhaps one day you come home to a note on the kitchen table and a half-empty wardrobe or receive a stomach-churning text one mid-week afternoon. It is rather like the poignant song by the late great Glen Campbell *By the time I get to Phoenix* with its third verse lyrics of:

By the time I make Oklahoma she'll be sleepin'
She'll turn softly and call my name out loud
And she'll cry just to think I'd really leave her
Tho' time and time I try to tell her so
She just didn't know I would really go.

Losing love is incredibly painful. We lose connection, we feel the deep wounds of rejection and abandonment that can trigger in many people pain stemming from their childhood too. Abandonment is a primal fear and for good reason. If a baby is abandoned, it will die. Also being blindsided and not seeing it coming makes you start to doubt your own judgment.

Some women become so enraged and fixated on the man who rejects or abandons her, that she can become unwell or even mentally unstable like the archetypal 'bunny boiler' from the movie *Fatal Attraction*. In this case, it is sad that Alex is stigmatised as the 'evil bitch' of the piece, as she clearly exhibits borderline personality disorder that her rejection after a short torrid affair exacerbates.

However, due to being rejected in love, even a sane person can become quite emotionally unstable and women especially have been known to lose their jobs, homes, families, health, money, sanity and even their freedom (think of *Crimes of Passion*) due to this hurt that is compounded by their inability to let go.

This is the saving grace. Learning to 'let go' and doing so in a manner and time frame that leaves you with your sanity and self-respect still intact is key. At such times, one needs to find ways and support to get over the hurt and focus on a new future.

During the early stages of a relationship when you really want him or her to contact you as you are in the infatuation phase, you have to consciously hold back and give them and the relationship space to grow. If you have been abandoned, you cannot go around your feelings. You have to go through them. This means, when it is over, being able to mourn it and let go just like a bereavement. After all, your plans for the future have been terminated. You may start to question how you felt about the past and you will be raw about feeling, temporarily, not good enough. You may also crave their touch and times of intimacy. Understand and treat this like a death. There are stages of grieving (denial, anger, despair and acceptance), but bear in mind that this has to be got over without the former object of your desire. You cannot aim these emotions, like armed weapons, in their direction or it will become a downward spiral towards the sorts of bunny boiling behaviours that no one wants to embrace.

To move on, you need to adopt good behaviours. Walk in nature, indulge yourself, go away to see friends or discover a new place, start a new hobby or pick up an old one that you have neglected, write a journal, dance and start to live again. Be kind to yourself and remind yourself every day that you are enough by writing 'I Am Enough' on your mirrors in lipstick (or removable marker pen), and when the pain of loss has subsided and you have reclaimed your future, be very specific about who you want to manifest into your life. Write down the values and attributes of your ideal partner and perhaps break old patterns of behaviour by making the unfamiliar familiar. If you have been attracted to ambivalent, alpha, good-looking partners then look beyond the outer wrapping and be open to dating someone who is perhaps less perfect on the outside but is emotionally mature and capable of intimacy (seeing into you the heart and soul of you and accepting you for who you are) and lasting healthy relationships.

Reset! A Blueprint for a Better Life

Above all, create a healthy relationship with yourself. Develop an ability to give and receive love, starting with you and if you actively engage in loving yourself and, to the best of your ability, loving all those who cross your path (or at least seeing the best in them or moving on), you will grow. Ghandi said: "Be the change you want to see in the world" and this is never more true than for close intimate relationships. If you want to attract someone marvellous, you have to become an equal match and develop all the wonderful qualities you seek in a mate in yourself. Also take action along the way. It is not only when you have love or an intimate relationship that you get to do loving and intimate things. Do them anyway, for yourself or deserving others. Be the change, the person and the actions that you want to attract. This is called 'Mirroring' and is based on the premise that the universe reflects back onto you what you put out.

The alternative can be fatal.

Lou Reed's *It's a Perfect Day* sounds like the best day ever, with a trip to the zoo and other pastimes. It is about cocaine. If all else fails, have a relationship with that and you can have a perfect day. Sadly, that perfect day is an illusion and runs on borrowed time before you have a very imperfect day and a highly imperfect future.

Societal pressure and what you can do to escape it

Women, as mentioned earlier, are often taught by society to be people-pleasers. I can't listen to the Sunday morning radio request programmes anymore. They are on my 'Stop doing' list. Every other request seems to run along the lines of: "She is a wonderful wife, mother, gran. I never tell her how much I love her and how lucky I am to have her. Nothing is too much trouble. She puts us all before herself and we all want to wish her a lovely day." While that is a lovely sentiment, I can only hear that this woman has paid a very high price for her ticket. Her ticket to being appreciated as the perfect wife/mother, etc, is that she has never put herself first. She has put others before herself for so long that she probably barely knows what would make her happy. I'm sure that the kind radio request and the lovely day with lunch and flowers will make her happy, but why should she be lauded for being the one to always sacrifice herself and infrequently get thanked for it?

This will be a contentious point here for many. If you are reading this and love nothing more than making your family happy then you are blessed as you have found your true worth and life purpose. However, I meet countless women who are exhausted. Disconnected with themselves. They don't like the way they look or how much they weigh. They feel that they can't say no to the request to have their grandchild every week as they know how much their son or daughter is struggling with their job and childcare costs. Perhaps they long to see their other son but he only comes at Christmas as he is far away with a demanding job too. They can't remember the last time they had passionate spontaneous sex or even the energy to want it. Jack Nicholson's words are ringing in their ears: "Is this as good as it gets?"

I intuitively came up with an analogy that I have discovered is used by many therapists, as I will tell women who seem unable to stop being 'people pleasers' of the in-flight safety instructions: "In the event of an emergency, oxygen masks will drop from the overhead lockers and parents must attach their own mask before assisting children." An unconscious parent is a risk to a child in a decompressed cabin. An exhausted mother who thinks that putting herself first or saying no is not available to her is in danger of suffocation all the time. At risk of not being there, being present, being available, for her children or others in her life. The overwhelm will lead her to snap at them and then hate herself for it. The exhaustion will seriously compromise her health, her joy, her connection to her partner, children and significant others. It will fracture her most precious bond: her connection to herself. She may turn to external things to push down the tide of panic or pain such as food or alcohol or antidepressants. Just numb it all and all because she was conditioned to think that selflessness was a virtue.

Men and women can please their parents in their choice of career and then hate it. Again and again I see people who have trained as a doctor or accountant or similar 'desired career' because it was what their parents valued either due to their culture or own experiences or aspirations. They will share sentiments such as: "My father is an accountant. He didn't allow me to go to drama school as he said it would be a waste of time and money. So I'm an accountant and I hate getting up and going to work every day." "I'm good at my job, but there is a side of me that is creative and crying out for expression. I feel I'm not authentic. It's all a sham."

"Not following your heart's desire is the major
cause of depression." - Marisa Peer.

Given the huge cost of university today, I can understand that parents, in an attempt to be helpful and give good guidance, will steer their offspring away from 'frivolous' degrees and courses, but there has to be balance. If your child is just putting off a job for three years by studying Armenian Media in the 20th century or some other rather eclectic subject, then put the whole university plan on the 'Stop doing' list. Instead, why not help them to travel the world, work overseas or become an intern at a charity or NGO while they tap into their passions and calling? Your children's happiness is a win/win situation for you too so let them have their freedom to choose. Perhaps to allow them to study for a degree of their choosing. There is much evidence that adults who pursued a degree that reflected their interests are happier in the long term. It is certainly the case for me. I studied English Literature. Three years reading all the great classics of world literature that still fire me up, comfort and delight me today, and I learned so much about history and human psychology whilst loving words and the imagination. All factors that have influenced positively my life and career choices.

Since 2000, Gallup has polled millions of employees from nearly 200 countries around the world about their level of job satisfaction. According to its findings in 2017, 85% of workers worldwide admit to hating their jobs when surveyed anonymously. "Many people in the world hate their job and especially their boss," the report says.

The state of the economy doesn't help, but the most influential factor is that a large percentage of workers are uninterested, uninspired and unfulfilled by their jobs. Like the whining dog, they may stay out of fear of change or the risk to their level of security. They may simply be confused about what a fulfilling change would look like. They have been settling for so long that they can no longer remember what they are passionate about.

If this is you, take a moment to recall what you imagined yourself doing before you started the grind? You did this earlier, so go back or rethink it now. When you were a child aged between 8 and 15, what did you love to do? What did you

Reset! A Blueprint for a Better Life

dream of becoming? It is not too late to pursue your dreams. Doing something you love will make you more fulfilled and happy than any job title or large pay cheque can ever deliver. It is easy to take career advice or think about transferable skills. So having more than one career, or life for that matter, and reinventing yourself several times over is a choice that is available to you. I was not unhappy in my former career of PR/Marketing/Communications but realised that I had many transferable skills to take into the world of therapy including being able to create rapport with people; read people; communicate effectively both verbally and in writing; problem solve and be responsive. Plus, be able to build a business.

There are numerous career tests that can help you to really understand your aptitudes and perhaps suggest new jobs or careers that would build on your skills and yet allow you to follow your passions.

As Confucius said: "Choose a job you love and you will never have to work a day in your life."

Many anorexics don't want to grow up on a subconscious level. They often have high-flying parents who love them, but may put pressure on them to achieve, often in no other way than just by the living example of their daily lives. A creative, sensitive child whose parents live life in the fast lane may just feel a huge weight of expectation of this being the life they are expected to lead. It can become overwhelming and often if they try to express themselves it is not heard. So their best form of control is to control their food intake. Contrary to popular belief, anorexics like food. They usually know more about calories and nutrition than many so-called experts. They may spend hours preparing healthy food each day. Only to leave most in the fridge. Severe anorexia in girls takes them back to being a smaller, non-hormonal (periods will usually stop) version of themselves. Perhaps to stay as Daddy's little girl. At least to stop the scary progression towards adulthood and the resulting pressures of expectation.

The therapeutic solution to such issues has to be tailored to each individual, but on the whole it is to allow them to be themselves, to feel once again that their desires for their life and what makes them tick is valid and attainable. That they are good enough. That they can learn to love themselves again and be loved for who they are and that that is enough. That they can have dreams and start to feel empowered enough to go after them. Not to be a carbon copy of anyone else or to have to please others by their behaviour, or even to let go of the need to rebel in order to be seen. In short, that they can control so much more of their lives in this way. Once they have a purpose and a sense of self-worth it will be natural to want to live and be healthy and so eating more food that sustains their body and mind will be a natural way forward.

In the words of the brilliant Ester Perel: "They want to be seen. They want to understand what motivates them and follow that passion. They want Intimacy or 'Into Me See'. To look inside themselves and love it. To let others look inside them and in return look into that person. The act of seeing and feeling that person at their most open and honest level creates a level of deep and honest connection that enhances their relationship."

Find Your True Values

We experience greater happiness if we live by our values. 'To thine own self be true' is the mantra, but so many people, including myself in the past, wonder just what exactly are their true values. What is at the core of their being and drives them onwards? There are many useful exercises for discovering your true values including looking down a list of core values, highlighting the ones that stand out to you, bunching them together (for example, if you have chosen a number of words such as Happy, Joy, Fun, Enjoyment, Optimism, etc, then they will clearly go together). Once you have chunked them down into about five categories you then choose the one word that resonates with you the most.

However, you need to live your words and they need to move you.

So when I'm coaching people I ask them to think about a life of wealth and balance that includes the Five F's of Faith, Fitness, Family, Friends and Finance.

Against each category ask yourself what you believe to be true about it? For example, if you believe that 'Fitness is something that will always be compromised for me as I was ill as a child', then you are not going to act as if peak fitness is available to you. Perhaps it isn't available to you. Perhaps it is and it is just your belief about it that stops you from really being the best you can be.

There is no right or wrong here just scribble down what you believe.

On a scale of 1 – 10 (with 10 being the absolute best place to be) rank this in your life right now.

Perhaps it is a 6/10 or a 7/10? Once you have this score, ask yourself: "What would be my overarching goal here, if I were to create the health of my dreams? To be a 10/10?" Perhaps this would be something like "If I were totally fit then I'd have more energy, feel better about my body so be sexier and love life better".

This is getting to your 'why', so now ask yourself: "Why is it important for me to have better, uncompromised health?" The answers here could be to do with what you want (such as feeling sexy) and what you don't want, such as having to take time off work as you keep picking up colds, or being unable to go on long walks as your back hurts too much.

Repeating this exercise across all the five categories will then give you a values list that is true to you and that moves you to want to live by these values or improve them. Keep it handy and remind yourself of it daily. If you have to make a decision about something important, for example a new relationship, ask yourself if it fits with your values? If you have a value of 'My faith is key to my life and who I am and I will meditate/pray/visit the temple, etc, every day to be at one with my God' then hooking up with an atheist is probably not going to work well unless you both have an amazing ability to respect and live with each others' points of view.

CHAPTER FOUR

Find the power of NO

"There is nothing noble in being superior to your fellow men. True nobility lies in being superior to your former self."

Ernest Hemingway

The British are notorious for saying sorry and we often apologise for other people's mistakes, such as being bumped into.

There is nothing wrong with good manners, but to always be feeling apologetic means you are not in your own power. You are probably very bad at saying "no", which is why the 'Suffocated Squeezed Suffragette Syndrome' kicks in for so many women. The counterbalance is to have a 'Start saying NO to' list.

For starters, this can include the likes of:

NO to toxic people: the ones who drain you of time and energy because it is always about them and their drama or their need to always be in control. These psychic vampires can literally drain the life from you. If you suffer from fatigue or headaches, keep a note of who you are spending your time with. Sadly, the worst energy robbers can often be those closest to us. If you realise this, then you have one of two choices: put distance between you and remove yourself from their presence, or create a protective shield around yourself that helps to make you resistant to their ability to suck your life force from you.

NO to Frenemies: especially those who seem to love to tell you when you are wrong/screwing up again or look awful, as if this is some sort of helpful therapy for you.

NO to physical pain: if you have a physical condition that ranges from mildly discomforting to debilitating, the greatest gift you can give yourself is to at the very least manage and relieve this condition, or at best cure it. While tablets and medical treatments should not be discounted, especially for acute conditions, they can start to be counterproductive over a period of time. The very 'cures' themselves can bring side-effects, and let's face it, there are no 'side' effects. Only 'effects' and unwelcome ones. If you read the list of contraindications for most tablets, you realise just how debilitating these effects can be. It is not uncommon for people, for example, my late father following his stroke, to be on a cocktail of tablets, many of which are treating the effects of the other tablets. All these alien chemicals in your body put your vital organs under stress as they try to expel them or balance the body. Much physical pain can be cured through renegotiating with your brain.

NO to being wired by beliefs that are not working for you and are often not even your own. Recently a lovely lady announced to me that she could not go on a long trip to Australia because of her morbid fear of snakes. For good measure she added: "My mother passed this on to me." It reminded me of a wonderful question my son asked me when we were living in the Bahamas and he was eight years old. "Mummy", he said, "If two white people who live in the Bahamas and have good tans have a baby together, does the baby come out with a tan?" I explained that the answer was no. It was a sweet question and it made me laugh, and yet so many of us believe in things that we were brought up hearing. It is as if our parents' views, like metaphorical 'tans', are automatically passed on. Without question, we take on the beliefs, fears or even phobias of our parents. For example, I hear phrases from clients such as: "My father believed that if you had sex before marriage you would go to hell." This is a strong belief and religious beliefs are some of the strongest known to man. I would question: "Do you believe that? Have you questioned that belief? How is living with that belief working for you?" When we question beliefs, we can take away their power and hold. Just look at any dictatorship or extreme regime. The first thing that happens is that freedom of speech and the freedom to think is shut down. Don't be your own dictator and shut down your own freedom to think and create the beliefs that work for you. Other roles are available. Other beliefs are available and they will create you and your life.

NO to saying no to yourself. My son went for a new job a while ago. He is a very talented and hardworking chef. He had been loyal to his employers for several years, often in difficult conditions. As we were talking through his upcoming interview, he mentioned that he would be seeking the same salary as he was already on because "I don't have experience in catering functions for more than 50 people". I asked if they did many of these. "Some" came the reply. I asked him, "Who told you that because of this you couldn't be paid more, especially with all your fine dining experience and good work record?" "Not sure" he replied. I said that I thought that the population of the world is approximately 7.5 billion people and that the only person saying this to him is, well, he himself. He laughed.

He got the job with a better rate of pay. He was saying 'no' to himself and elaborating it with a false belief or construct that made it seem plausible, even true. When I was growing up, my parents never told me that a girl from a Midlands town, born in a terraced street that was subsequently pulled down, who attended a giant comprehensive couldn't do anything she wanted. So I never said no to myself. That is why my PR career in the 80s took off in the way it did. That is why I founded my own PR Company at the age of 29. No one was saying no, certainly not me, and if anyone was saying: "Oh you can't do that... because ..." I was not letting it in. In fact, it often galvanised me to prove them wrong.

NO to your old stories. I love stories – oral history is what mankind is founded on. Take a screenwriting course and deconstruct what makes a great movie (or book) and you find out that it is all about stories. The greatest speakers in the world, those with millions of clicks on TED Talks, etc, tell stories. The Bible. The Qur'an. The Tora. But what are the stories that you are telling yourself on a daily basis? Are you now in your 60s and still sticking to the old story of "I can never truly be happy because of my terrible childhood"?

I dealt with a wonderful man in his late 70s. All his life he had been unable to use not only public toilets but pretty much any toilet away from home. As he aged and his need to go to the toilet more frequently became an issue, he became almost housebound, afraid to go out. Hypnotic regression let him access a story his subconscious was telling him repeatedly that had been triggered by a shaming incident in the toilets at school and a domineering father at home. This was about 50 years out of date and no longer serving him. As discussed earlier, the past is a construct, and your mind or memory of it will create its own reality for you particularly if you play the scenes over and over again, investing more colour and drama and life into your story with each passing day.

Reset! A Blueprint for a Better Life

If you have ever revisited your infant or kindergarten school, you will discover a few things. Firstly, the chairs are very small and so are the rooms. Secondly, the layout is not as you remembered it. The passageway from your classroom to the lunch room or Head Teacher's office is probably short and boring and not the 'hall of terror' from your memory. It was all about perspective at the time. When you were only five years old, those chairs were a lot bigger in relation to you. When you had to walk to the lunch room and that cruel boy would shout 'four eyes' or similar at you, then that corridor became a place of fear, but now it is only continuing to be big and fearful in your mind. Not in reality.

NO to not daring to have the life you want and deserve. To opening your heart. To taking risks. In her brilliant book *Daring Greatly* (that I recommend to many of my clients), Brené Brown speaks from personal experience and how, following her breakdown, she learned that being vulnerable and open is the greatest strength you can have. She speaks about 'wholehearted' people who are able to engage with the world from a place of openness, even if loving in such a way means you get your heart broken. Because the opposite is to stay shut. To shut down your heart and cut yourself off from others and joy because you are afraid of being hurt. No one likes being hurt.

Remember we are wired to avoid pain and seek pleasure. We are wired to seek connection and avoid rejection, but the price of the ticket can be so high that we get the opposite of what we desire. Such as: "I want love and connection and the status of a marriage so the fact that Jim hits me when he has too much to drink is OK. He doesn't mean it. Look at our lovely house and he is such a good dad. He loves me. I will stay." The character of Celeste Wright in the powerful American drama series *Big*

Little Lies is played by Nicole Kidman. Celeste looks to have the most perfect life and incredible marriage to a sexy younger man who adores her. They have two blond, beautiful boys. A beachside house. She has amazing looks and body. She has friends. She seems to have a passionate sex life too until we lift the veil over the series and see into the dark reality of her world. That she is an abused wife.

Nicole Kidman won an Emmy award for her performance, and on accepting her award she spoke out on the need to recognise hidden abuse saying: "It is in this role that I come to fully understand the barriers that women around the world are facing. I have focused on lending my voice to women who are survivors of violence. The stories I have heard from them have shaken me to the core and changed me forever. More than ever, I am aware of the need to support and celebrate each other."

NO to staying stuck because you just don't know what you want. Take a piece of paper and draw a box on it that is just a little smaller than the paper when placed vertically. Outside the box on the top left hand side write: In my life now. On the right hand side write: Not in my life now. On the left hand side outside the box at the bottom write: Don't Want. At the top write: Want. Then draw a line across the middle of this internal box to create four boxes. Then sit quietly. Relax. Breathe. Think about your life now and the life you want to visualise or get a feeling about and fill in the boxes. Drill down in this exercise by taking the items in the top right hand box ('Not in my life now' that I want!) and make an availability list. If, for example, in this box you have 'A clean and tidy and calm home environment' then list what is available to you now. A cleaner perhaps? You may start to tell the story of 'I just can't afford that', but can you if you put something on your 'not doing' list such as 'Stop drinking half a bottle of wine each weekday evening'? This is a win/win situation. You will resolve to stop buying at least three bottles of wine each week and the money you save can pay for a cleaner once a month. If, for example, in this box you have: 'A partner of my dreams' but you are questioning whether they will truly be available, then you need to make a 'Let's make it available list'. A little effort and planning for a great reward.

Clearly it is difficult to meet new people once you are past your 20s or 30s as you don't go for drinks after work regularly or go to nightclubs or parties or weddings. Having done a review of where all my baby boomer friends met their partners, this was pretty much it. I suppose there are also festivals today, but for those of us above 40 this isn't always possible, or desirable to be honest.

So where are those people hiding that you could have a new and wonderful relationship with? Well probably on an online dating site. They are hidden in plain view out there on the internet. From personal experience in this arena I can offer the following advice: firstly, choose a dating site that fits with your values and personality.

I would suggest that if you want a life partner, especially if you are in your 40s and beyond, that you give Tinder a miss and even steer clear of some of the large-scale free matching sites. There are just too many opportunists out there. It will take ages to sift through the players to get to 'the one'. I've written an article on this topic, so I don't want to scare you with the stories of how many married people (men mostly) use these sites to meet rather vulnerable women. I don't do scared. So just avoid the cattle markets.

If, for example, you would like to share your love of golf with a special someone, then check out dating sites for single golfers. Even if the chemistry isn't there, you may spend an enjoyable half day playing nine holes, improving your handicap, and possibly find a new golf partner. Similarly, for YogaRomance. This is a free site, and I actually like its format that asks for your favourite book, movie and music. That tells you a lot about a person and you already know you both like yoga. Personally I've found the most genuine, open and decent men on Muddy Matches. It seems that those who like the country, long walks, fresh air and animals tend to have their egos in check. Once you start to join these particular dots you can see how being focused about what you want or don't want and approaching it with the belief that everything is possible and available can make it all straightforward and doable. Exciting even. Vulnerable to be sure. Worth it in the long run.

And here is some personal guidance for you when you are on that journey. For starters, have some good support around you. This is important as you may start to question your own judgment when you mistakenly feel like you have 'got it wrong'.

I've had long, wonderful lunches filled with laughter and lots of things in common and then, nothing. No follow up. My upbeat text ignored, or my What's App message unread, meaning I'm either blocked or they have just gone AWOL. Or perhaps you get to date three, even four, and it gets more intimate, even physical, and again, nothing. You torture yourself by checking the dating site and see they were active earlier that day. Not always a bad sign, as the algorithms of the sites target you increasingly the less you visit by throwing up a 'match' or new 'fan' that you are often curious to check out.

That is why you need that good support. Some caring friends or family or neighbours who can let you cry on their shoulder or are great for getting you out and about. I have friends who tell me to put on my walking boots and then we go for long uplifting walks together. Others to share a bottle of wine with (although be careful not to make this your default setting for obvious health reasons), cinema friends, theatre buddies, etc.

Perhaps you actually realise that you still need to work on yourself, love yourself more and not feel the need to be completed by a relationship so shelve the whole search process for a while. Put it in (temporarily) the part of the grid that lists: 'In my life now and don't want' box.

All the items in this box then need to go straight onto your 'Stop doing list'.

NO to being limitless. The movie, *Limitless*, is actually based on some truth. There is a drug, Modafinil, which was created as a medical helper for people who suffer from narcolepsy. If you suffer from narcolepsy, you suffer from the inability to stay awake throughout the day without suddenly falling asleep. Dave Asprey of BulletProof coffee fame (who I've met and I drink Bulletproof Coffee, so I hold in some esteem) has used Modafinil for many years and says it has improved his life. Dave still uses it occasionally although he says that he doesn't need it any more. It is a nootropic – a drug that enhances your natural abilities or performance (this time to get more done and focus more). According to Dr Scott Vrecko, nootropics might not increase a person's ability to receive, remember or process information; instead, they will have a positive effect on a person's mood while performing these tasks. Vrecko spent a few weeks at an American university collecting testimonies from students and many said that the pill made them feel more capable of performing their tasks – even before they got started. Another study points out that Modafinil could induce a state of excessive confidence. Personally I've not tried it. I can see the attraction for students or those facing ridiculous deadlines (I recall once working 24 hours straight through in my PR Agency days to prepare, present and win a pitch). My caveat is that we are not limitless. If you try to push through your natural boundaries, sleep patterns and energy levels on a regular basis, then you will find you are the opposite of limitless. Let's remember that we are human beings, not human doings.

NO to believing it is not possible. On the flipside of taking a Limitless pill is a pill that openly tells you that it is a placebo. A very interesting company called Xpill tells you that its (rather unimaginatively named) Xpill can help you to change your life, to become limitless, and that this pill is a placebo and basically a super vitamin tablet. I attended a seminar where someone took one on stage with a glass of water. Before they swallowed this pill they made a commitment to what it would change within them; from memory I believe the young woman wanted to summon up the courage to make a country move to a new life. What the organisation behind Xpill has realised is that it is the intention, the visualisation and public commitment to your goal and dream that is important. The pill is a symbol of this. I've received a few newsletter updates from Xpill, and this lady made her move and many others have followed through on their vows. Perhaps we just need a physical representation or marker of those intentions?

Like Roger Bannister and all athletes who set Personal Bests and then better them, you can set and raise your 'Limit Level'. Just like all those who beat the four-minute mile because they knew it was possible (or limitless), you can do the same. For starters, just decide to make a difference. If you Google 'How to improve your life', there are thousands of answers and courses and promises. 'You can take your life back in five easy steps. Just follow my programme.' 'The five sure ways to gain success, every day.' '12 Life Hacks that will make you unstoppable', etc.

Who isn't tempted by such promises? It can seem overwhelming and the dilemma is how do you sort out the wheat from the chaff? Having worked in close quarters with some of the world's leading personal development gurus, and attended across three decades and more continents the leading seminars and workshops available, I have some good insight here. What is your level? If it is entry level, weekend workshops such as Tony Robbins' Unleash the Power Within is pretty inspiring and will certainly fire you up. Events such as A-Fest and courses including LifeBook are a big investment of time and money and self-belief, but if you are ready for them and at a level that is nearing self-actualisation, then I would recommend them too. MindValley, HayHouse, Deepak and Oprah and Udemy have dozens of accessible online courses that you can follow, as does the inexpensive yet good quality DailyOm.

Say NO to a chaotic day. I love to start each day with a message from The Universe that is a short nugget of wisdom tailored to you (after you fill in a form with some preferences). It will make you smile. **http://www.tut.com/account/register** I also meditate every day unless I'm travelling and on a different time zone. Meditation allows me to quiet my mind. I find that guided meditations are best as they stop the mind chatter from coming back in. The mind thinks involuntarily just like the heart beats involuntarily, so trying to command it to stop thinking is like trying to stop your heart from beating unless you get some tools to help you. I used to lay awake at night with a non-stop chatter of thoughts and an endless mind full of a 'to-do' list taking the place of sleep. My body held so much stress that I had a number of stress-related illnesses. Using one of the many guided meditations I have uploaded on my phone, wearing wireless headphones, I start the day by taking 10 to 20 minutes to bring my awareness into that present moment and fill my head with positive thoughts. I use square breathing too, where you breathe in for four counts, hold it for four counts, breathe out for four counts and again hold it for four counts. This combination allows me to let go and face the day ahead in a more positive way and with increased energy.

At the end of this book is a glossary of books that I recommend repeatedly to my clients. These too can be great, and if you don't think you can make the time to read, buy an audio book. Listen while you drive, garden or walk.

Of course, hypnosis tapes are key. My own range is growing and you can find the links in this book. There is the excellent Marisa Peer, and for meditations I love Belleruth Naparstak – I was given her *Guided Meditation During Surgery* CD when I had the cancer years ago and it helped me to sail through the operation and be sitting up with a cup of tea only 20 minutes after waking up.

What is really important is to embrace these ideas that will push you beyond your 'Limit Level'. Think about mentors (alive, dead, real or imaginary) who could guide you in this process. Create a 'Sounding Board'. A board of imaginary mentors who you can turn to for inspiration or guidance. For example, let's say you want to set up a children's play scheme. Walt Disney would have something to say about that. Have Walt on your

'Sounding Board'. Invite him in your planning process to a meeting. "So Walt, I was thinking that the play scheme could be all based on frogs. They are part of the cycle of life and I like them. What do you think?" Hear what he'd say in your mind.

You can of course involve real people. Who do you respect in your family, community, circle of friends? No one springs to mind? Then join one of the many business breakfast clubs, or networking associations, where the sharing of ideas, mutual support for business development and training are all regular and important activities.

Whatever you choose to do, be mindful of a few things.

Firstly, have a goal for each of these activities or you can become a course or group junkie and just enjoy the buzz and camaraderie of the courses for their own sake. This is fine if you are a retired multi-millionaire who is tired of sipping pink gin with a nice view and craves connection, growth and fulfilment. If this is you, go for it! Otherwise think about what your outcome is.

Also be aware of the rule of C.A.N.I. - Constant and Never Ending Improvement. Like a PB (personal best). This moves onwards and upwards each time you reach a new goal or limit. That way you are limitless, in the best way possible, without the need for medication.

CHAPTER FIVE

Change the voice in your head and the face looking back at you in the mirror

Young souls learn to accept responsibility for their actions. Mature souls learn to accept responsibility for their thoughts. And old souls, Rosalyn, learn to accept responsibility for their happiness.

Weeeeeeee,
The Universe

My late mother had lovely skin and thankfully I do too. All her life she washed her face in soap and water and used cold cream or Oil of Ulay (as it then was). Sometimes she would put olive oil on her hair and skin. She didn't know about photo damage, weakened collagen, age spots and premature ageing. When she got the Avon catalogue her choice of skin care did not come with the words 'Age Defying', nor was it set out for the over 30s/40s/50s woman. Of course, people have always aged, but we are now surrounded by an industry that 'addresses the visible signs of ageing' as if it were a curse. That treats changes in our lives, such as the menopause, as if they are medical problems.

In addition to a bewildering range of skin creams with the likes of bee venom, minerals, charcoal or Vitamins E and C and Q10 there are new anti-ageing potions launched every day. Most recently one that you can drink: Anti-AGin – a gin that is distilled with drinkable collagen; and from Cambridge scientists you may now partake of a few slabs of Esthecho: dark chocolate with anti-ageing properties.

Then there are the exercise and diet regimes. Oxygen therapy. Anti-oxidants. Botox, fillers, chemical peels, half-face lifts, face lifts and eye lifts. You can even have your bottom enhanced or create a designer vagina.

Many treatments have validity but the most powerful anti-ageing tool is the mind.

Believing in your choice of exercise and anti-ageing so that your mind supports the changes to your body is key. If all the time you are applying a cream to your face that costs more than your weekly shop while saying: "Well, this will just be another waste of money, I look so old", then guess what, it will fail. This is the basis of the Law of Attraction.

For starters, change the voice in your head. Now if I look in the mirror and the critical voice starts, I change it to, "I look tired. A juice for breakfast is a good idea and let's get lots of fresh air today and go to bed on time." Much kinder and more helpful. Not to mention cheaper.

Changing your thinking does not require the hard effort that changing your body through exercise does. Small adjustments to the voice inside your head are key, and the secret is to not let in societal mantras about ageing.

Older mothers are a perfect example. While there is no debate that a woman's peak fertility is in her 20s, there is also no rule, other than the one we have developed in the West, about women over 40 not being able to conceive naturally. The label 'Geriatric Pregnancy' is given to any woman having a child above the age of 35, although it is more often replaced with the rather kinder term 'Advanced Maternal Age'.

Women of 35 and above are offered a barrage of tests due to the risks of an 'imperfect' pregnancy or baby. Yet tribal cultures don't know this. They will have children as long as they are able. The Victorians didn't know this. They would have children over a 20-year period meaning that many would have been conceived when the mother was well into her 40s. Celebrity Mums don't accept this. Celebrities definitely do things differently but one of the key things that they do is not allow society to tell them that they can't do something. Clearly Halle Berry, Madonna, Uma Thurman, Mariah Carey and Celine Dion have decided that not only are Oscars and amazing and long careers available to them, but also babies.

Did you know that the Queen sends out 18 times as many 100-Year Birthday telegrams as she did when she ascended to the throne in 1952?

The truth is, we are now living for longer. So we are older for longer. Former ideas of what age and retirement looked like are being rejected daily as the baby boomer generation (those born between 1946 and 1964 in the boom of having babies in the post-war (WW2) years) step into the territory once marked as 'old'. Fifty thousand people turn 50 each week in the UK and by 2020 the over 50s will represent in excess of 50% of the UK population.

Being savvy about advertising, baby boomers demand information not hype, and up to 86% believe that advertising is not relevant to them. Hardly surprising when you realise that the average age of an advertising executive in the UK is 33 and only 5.6% of those who work in the UK advertising industry is aged over 50. So Adland is full of a mindset that all new cars and funky fashion should be sold to the younger consumer. Not the ones who have the money: the 50+ market.

Baby boomers can pay for it and they demand choice. They demand individualisation – having gone on package holidays since the 1960s, this is the generation that is leading the way in adventure and personalised holidays. There is also a growth in 'gap year' 50+ and 'World Nomads' (people who only have a small bolthole somewhere, if at all, and travel and meet up with other like-minded individuals in the pursuit of personal development). Often this has a strong philanthropic side with people setting up their own charities or fundraising programmes.

Not surprisingly, those who do 'traditional' activities do them in their own way. Baby boomers lead the way in writing their own marriage vows. They also lead the way in writing their own funeral rites and planning their goodbyes. The biggest sale of Harley Davidsons and convertible cars are to the 50+ market. Over 50s spend a greater share of the nation's income than any other group and they are now the UK's 9th biggest mortgage borrowers. The Bank of Mum and Dad is now nearly as powerful as Barclays and a lot more flexible and human no doubt.

So why is it that when I turned 50, the Saga and Innovations catalogue landed on my doorstep? As I contemplated a new tattoo and internet dating, someone thought I'd like an adjustable bath rail and Velcro shoes. No, the New Old don't look like the Old Old. My sister and I recently realised that a much-cherished black and white photograph of us holding hands with our grandmas as we strolled along the seafront at Sutton-on-Sea depicted two women who were younger than we are today. They have grey permed hair, long flowery dresses, granny sandals and, although unseen, I remember the bloomers and other terrible undergarments. We look nothing like that. We feel nothing like that, as if life is already in its closing stages and that feeling sexy or attractive is taboo.

There is already a backlash against those 'anti-ageing' creams and potions. Why shouldn't we want to age? The alternative doesn't bear thinking about. The beauty brands Dove and Kiel's (with its Act Any Age campaign) are getting it right. They show women who are not afraid to show their bodies and personalities in their later age. Perhaps that is why another interesting statistic is that the biggest rise in naturists is among the over 50s.

What is now truer than ever before is that age is a state of mind. Glastonbury and music festivals are now multi-generational as the grandparents, parents and kids all share a trendy yurt together. The Rolling Stones still tour. Mick Jagger does the equivalent of a marathon on stage every night and no one has told him he is old. So he doesn't think it and he doesn't act it. He is not immature or hedonistic. Just vital.

In a huge survey by Sun Life, 72% of men aged between 75 and 85 said that a satisfactory sex life is crucial to maintaining a relationship. 85% of retirees felt that they retired too early and a fifth who retired went on to get another job. 60% eat healthily and 58% keep their mind active. The other 42% need to get on board with this one. It's not just doing the crossword or Sudoku that will make the difference, but having a mindset that reaching age 50 is literally the 50% mark. A staging post to the next 50 years of life, organisations such as U3A (University of the 3rd Age) and clubs give this group life-long learning and connecting.

In primitive societies, ageing was and still is, valued. In the West, the mindset is changing from seeing ageing as becoming infirm and dying to a new and rewarding third age in our lives. Older people can be an enormous resource to their families and communities. However, they may end up in the 'Squeezed Middle', meeting both the needs of ageing parents and children who are at school or university, or they may be providing care to grandchildren and be stuck in a 'Double Sandwich'.

My own mantra is that 'Life is full of endless possibilities'. When I was diagnosed with breast cancer, the hospital experts, particularly the oncologist, threw a great number of statistics at me about my probabilities for survival, etc.

My questions, own research and listening to my heart about what was right for me put me in control, and my mantra was 'I'm not a statistic. I'm not the norm. Why should I let that in?'

I had the privilege of hearing Celebrity Nutrition and Fitness expert JJ Virgin speak and share her story about how she defied 100-to-one odds of her son surviving. In her own words she says:

"On a narrow dark street, wearing black attire, my son never saw the car that struck him and left him for dead.

"After he was airlifted to a hospital, doctors grimly informed me they couldn't do anything for him. He was in a coma with bones literally sticking out of his body. One doctor grimly said, 'You have to let him go.'

94

"Anyone who has kids knows that letting them go isn't an option – not for one millisecond. If you can fight for them in any capacity, you fight. I determined, in that moment, to prove those doctors wrong.

"He was airlifted to the UCLA trauma center. In the intensive care unit, feeling completely powerless and out of control, I kept thinking to myself, 'I have to do something. I have to do something.'

"I knew I couldn't navigate this alone. I reached out to my rock star friends and colleagues, who happen to be among the best medical minds in the world.

"I also wrote a letter to my social media tribe. 'Monday evening the unfathomable happened', the letter began. I wasn't asking for sympathy. I wanted support. We talk about being 'real' and 'authentic', but getting vulnerable is a whole different game. Within minutes, I received texts, emails and phone calls from doctors, healers, top brain researchers and other health professionals asking what they could do.

"Grant survived surgery, but he remained in a coma. As I watched him that evening, I knew I would do whatever it took to make sure he became 110 per cent.

"While all of this unfolded, I had a book going to press. As my family's sole source of financial support, I couldn't let the launch slip, even though I sat in the intensive care unit 15 hours a day. So again, I reached out. I sent out an SOS to friends, affiliates and partners.

"Fast forward: Grant not only survived, but thrived. I don't use this word lightly, but he's a walking miracle and my book? The book debuted as a New York Times best-seller (and the launch made millions). After you almost lose a child, you see things

differently. Little things no longer feel like herculean battles. You clearly discover why health and wellness truly matters. I had to remain my best self to be there for Grant. The 'often traveled' route of not eating, sleeping, or taking care of oneself in a crisis was NOT the way to go. How could I truly show up and fight for Grant if I was collapsing?

"Understanding our self-worth – living intentionally, being our best selves, maintaining impeccable health – this gives us the capacity to transform our lives and those of the people we love."

Open any glossy magazine and there will be statistics along the lines of: "70% of women say that they XYZ". Ask yourself, which women? What day of the week did you ask them? Were biscuits or wine included if it was a focus group? Even the focus groups are skewed to get the desired results, they categorise and target the people who they ask to turn up. Often the types of people who volunteer to be in focus groups display what is known in psychology as a Volunteer Bias. This means that those who do show up will, by their very nature, be different from the general population. They are more likely to be outgoing, extroverted and more oriented towards the self.

So bearing in mind the questionable nature of statistics and 'odds' and the labels we are given about everything from our pregnancies to our diseases, isn't it time to evaluate if this is working for you?

If you are given the label of a disease, take time to evaluate the variability of the symptoms. Is this what you really have? Are you stuck with it forever? I was told at 26 that I had IBS and needed to take a drug every day for the rest of my life. I was offered chemotherapy at the time of the cancer. I was told that hearing loss would be a bonus for me as it would reduce the symptoms of the tinnitus. People I know were told they would never conceive and then when they did that they would never carry the baby to term. As they helped their daughter blow out 25 candles on her cake they rejoiced that they didn't let the words in.

I never spoke of 'being in remission', I simply did not let the word remission in – it implies that it is lurking and on hold and will probably come back. For me, the minute I woke up after the lumpectomy it was no longer there. Gone. Period. If someone healthy with no cells behaving badly was tested then they would be told they were cancer free, or if they met a milestone that the doctors imposed – 5 years or 10 years – then they would be told that they were cured. I decided to believe this from the outset and then did everything I could to support a full recovery.

If you would like still more proof about how the mind can change our bodies and even counter ageing, check out the Counterclockwise study.

In 1979, psychologist Ellen Langer from Harvard University conducted a unique experiment to find out what would happen when a group of eight older men were given the experience of living 20 years earlier. She and her team created a living environment complete with food, films and photos from the period. The group 'acted as if' it was 20 years earlier and discussed news, politics and sport in the present tense as if they had travelled back in time.

What is wonderful is that the group appeared physically and psychologically younger and changed their performances for the better on benchmark tests. Their hearing, grip strength and manual dexterity improved. Memory and IQ scores also improved. Because their minds were actively engaged in living

20 years earlier, their bodies seemed to follow. Ellen believes this is a demonstration of how our bodies don't let us down as we get older, it's our minds that accept the labels of ageing. Freeing ourselves from that state of mind can turn back the clock.

This experiment was replicated by the BBC in its programme *The Young Ones* when it filmed six well-loved celebrities in their 70s and 80s – Liz Smith, Lionel Blair, Dickie Bird, Sylvia Syms, Derek Jameson and Kenneth Kendall – who spent one week living as though it were their heyday – 1975 – to see if re-living your youth can make you young again.

Their country retreat was made up to be an authentic 1970s home, they wore the clothes of the 1970s, they cooked favourite dishes of the time and their pastimes included 70s TV, 70s video games and favourite LPs from the decade. Overseeing the experiment were Dr Michael Mosley and Ellen Langer. The results of the programme spoke for themselves. All the celebrities left with a new lease of life and Liz Smith was seen walking without her walking aid due the fact, as she put it, that she "forgot to be old". Another participant, Dickie Bird, was filmed after he left the house. He went out for a pub meal with a group of friends and they all commented on how much better he was looking. He added: "I know my memory, even for a 77 year old, was terrible. Now I'm sharper in my mind and I've got my confidence back. I'm glad I went. I can feel it's done something. It's certainly interesting that having this sort of experience can improve you. Perhaps they should have it on the National Health."

At the time of her original study, Ellen Langer said: "The problem is that the medical world has helped us see the word 'psychosomatic' as pretending. The symptoms are real. Now, if

Reset! A Blueprint for a Better Life

you see disease as in some ways guided by your thoughts and you know you have control over your thoughts, then that would mean that there's at least a modicum of control that we can exert over any of our diseases. I actually believe our minds have almost complete control over our diseases."

What is still a mindset blockage for many older people, women in particular, is admitting openly and seeking help when things are not right at home. There is growing evidence about a shocking amount of domestic abuse in older people (women in particular) with an estimated 120,000 individuals aged 65+ experiencing at least one form of abuse (psychological, physical, sexual or financial) in a recent one-year study (Multi-Agency Risk Assessment Conferences).

There are also a number of barriers in the reporting of this that have been highlighted. For example, in a study conducted by Beaulaurier et al (2007), participants spoke of how historically the home was perceived as private and "what went on there was behind closed doors". Participants also felt a sense of shame or embarrassment and as such kept their experiences 'hidden' from family, friends and neighbours. Says one 76-year-old woman: "It was behind doors a lot, you know what I mean, like mine was and in them days, years ago, there was nothing at all for us to turn to, you know."

Moreover, study participants also spoke of the absence of formal or informal networks in terms of potential support: "There was nothing for you [. . .] and my parents would say "you make your bed then lay there" really [. . .] so I got no support [. . .] so I think that is the problem and which made me accept that [the abuse] in a very funny kind of a way" (Participant 1: 63 years), or: "There was no point in calling the police, they'd come and he'd be in the cells and the next morning home again and I'd get it for reporting it" (Participant 8: 76 years).

The feelings of shame or embarrassment experienced by women during the occurrences of abuse often lasted into later life. A participant spoke of how she felt that older women needed to be 'given permission' to speak out and to understand that it was acceptable to disclose domestic abuse.

Remaining silent on this issue is the greatest and most insidious problem of all. If this resonates with you then speak up, ask for help and reset this terrible pattern.

CHAPTER SIX

Ways to be the best brand 'YOU' you can be

"The key is to keep company only with people who uplift you, whose presence calls forth your best."

Aristotle

Many companies use psychometric testing, or the Myers-Briggs Type Indicator˙ (MBTI˙) test which gives a snapshot of what motivates you, how you feel, whether you are intuitive, etc. It is a way of making the psychological types described by C.G. Jung understandable. It is a relatively straightforward test (and many free versions exist on the internet) that categorises everyone into one of 16 distinctive personality types based on your interests, reactions, values, motivations and skills.

What is good about such tests is that you can gain better insight into not only your strengths and weaknesses, but also those of others. Such mutual understanding can then lead to improved relationships with others at work. For example, if you are very extrovert and outgoing, you may sit in a meeting with someone very quiet and mistake their reluctance to jump into conversation as being that they have no opinions worth sharing. They may be a reflective type and as such could be a very safe pair of hands for the extroverts who literally form their opinions as they speak. As someone who can relate to this latter type, I'd argue that you need all sorts to make a strong team. Having someone willing to jump in and take charge and come up with a solution quickly can also be relevant and necessary.

So, playing to everyone's strengths is key, as is an understanding about what makes you tick, how you tend to react and how to work better with others.

Businesses always work out better ways to plan and behave. Yet those who work in corporations and spend huge amounts of time on training, development and detailed business plans fail to have a life plan. They wouldn't start a project without a project plan but have no blueprint for their life. Before we cover this in more detail in Chapter 7, let's take a moment to look at a snapshot of the key elements of an effective life plan. The easy to remember Five B's of a Better Life Plan comprise:

Belief
Blue sky thinking
Bait
Brand you
Bulletproof

Beliefs:

From the insights and exercises you have covered so far in this book, you should now be better positioned to question and reassess your beliefs, having a greater understanding of where they come from. Those beliefs that were forced upon you as a child by your parents, teachers or leaders were never yours in the first place, so you have assessed if they are working for you now. If they are, this is good. They are underpinning who you are. If they are not and you feel at odds with them, throw them out now. Cultivate a better belief. For example, if you have been pushing for business success and doing quite well, but feel uneasy about it, as the mantra in your head is that 'Money makes you evil', then discard that one immediately.

Blue sky thinking: is about taking the cap off your expectations, dreams and desires and asking yourself, 'What could my life look like if...', 'How could life be if there were no limits to what I could do?' And other limitless and great questions to disrupt complacent thinking, habits and results.

Bait: is about why you are even going to go after something in the first place. Why do you want to be CEO of your company, for example? You have to really have a strong 'why' in order to put up with long hours or stress and the pressures that would go with that one. Everyone's bait on their hook is different, but you do need to examine yours and see if it is strong enough to hold and land the catch you desire.

If your bait for wanting to be CEO is 'to finally make my father proud of me, as he always said I wouldn't amount to anything', then you may make it there just to show him, but you will not be happy about either the journey or the destination. Whilst being driven by this motivation, you may lose friends or even close family on the journey as your need to prove yourself may be obsessive and probably not very caring of others. Often, even when people achieve greatness, they are still not praised by parents who are not forthcoming or family members, so they never get that approval. I've heard of movie directors whose parents still criticise them. Their inability to give them unconditional love or praise is actually the problem, and acting like a child seeking approval all of your life and not receiving it can be highly emotionally damaging.

Brand you: is understanding and building upon the fact that you are your own brand. It is like lettering in candy rock at the English seaside. The name of the resort is written in the stick of rock, and if you cut it anywhere across its length, that name will still be spelt out inside: Skegness, Blackpool, Southsea or Torbay. The principle is the same. Each touch-point along its length reveals exactly the same identity. Being your own brand means that you have congruency: you are your authentic self and you are not hiding behind a mask. If you are self-employed, a trader or practitioner of any kind, everything about you is your brand, from how you answer the phone and reply to emails, to your logo and branding, livery on a vehicle or the way your premises look right through to how you look and behave.

How many times have you come across a tradesperson who has a super eye-catching logo, a flash local newspaper advert and bright livery on their van, usually promising something like 'Plumbing Solutions', only to ring them and get no reply? You might leave a message for them and days later they reply while they are out and about and don't have their diary with them. Not much of a solution at all for you, especially if your toilet is still leaking. All of that investment they have made in their 'brand' is wasted, as to you their brand is unreliable and unobtainable, so you are busy asking the neighbours for a word-of-mouth recommendation to find someone trustworthy whose word is their brand. They may not even have a business card, but that is not a recommendation either in the grand scheme of 'Brand You'.

My late father employed a gardener who did a brilliant job. All the neighbours wanted details about him. He didn't have cards or leaflets. He didn't even rip up pieces of paper, scribble his details on them and post them through their letterboxes.

He obtained no business from the neighbours, they all went elsewhere, and when I bumped into him a few months later and he said that business was a bit slow, I had to bite my tongue.

There will be days when the best your brand can do is dress up and show up. That means be reliable and turn up when you promise. Dress up means dress the part. A friend recently posted a picture on Facebook from a conference she was attending. In it Richard Branson is leaning over the stage cutting off a man's tie with scissors. I wasn't an attendee, but I can guess the context. It used to be called 'suited and booted' and of course many workplaces have dress codes.

So what is your degree of flexibility here? If you are now in business for yourself, reinventing yourself after being made redundant, semi-retiring, coming out of a divorce or other life change, take some time on your image too. There are some amazing image consultants who will work with you to cull your wardrobe and even shop with you to find clothes that suit your body shape, personality and desires. It may seem extravagant and throwing out 21 bin bags of clothes can be quite painful, but it is ultimately cathartic and liberating. I did it. I would open two crammed wardrobes and declare that I had nothing to wear, as many of the clothes didn't fit well, didn't flatter me and didn't go together. Now that is not a problem, and having fewer but better clothes also adds an extra dimension to your life. Simplicity and cutting down choice and dilemma allows you to focus more attention on the things you want to put your energy into and you usually look great too.

I've worked with some of the world's top movers and shakers and have observed that, on the whole, they do not have complicated lives in terms of the clothes they wear or the food they eat. They have 'restricted choice' in areas that are necessary, such as their wardrobe, and this allows them 'unrestricted choice' in other areas. They have a strong sense of image and brand so their look will not fluctuate wildly. Consequently, their wardrobes will contain many of the same or similar items, perhaps in different colours or fabrics. Their food, which has probably been developed as a peak performance diet to keep them filled with energy without empty calories, will be quite limited. I've opened their fridges. They are not filled with the sort of bewildering variety that some are. There will be several of the same item in different flavours; protein shakes, for example, or crudités and different types of dip.

Their brands go all the way through and when they don't, that is when trouble arises. There is a great quote that says: "Be the person your dog thinks you are." Another is: "Character is who you are when no one else is looking." This is the hard part. Being at one with yourself and your personal brand at all times. Not being a public figure such as a preacher and then getting caught out in a sting when you use call girls. It is hypocrisy, but it is also a very uncomfortable life to lead, as when you know in your heart that you are not your authentic self, it really hurts. On the other hand, when you are in alignment with your personal values, you feel happier, more at peace with yourself and your confidence increases. You sleep better. You are able to move towards your goals, as you have a strong grounding.

There are an overwhelming number of courses and methods to help people to un-tap their true potential and get back in touch with their authentic selves. Out of interest I signed up to many online until I realised I was spending up to 20 minutes a day just sifting through emails that all promised to 'Change your life in 30 days' or similar. Yet I hear the yearning from people asking to tap into their authentic selves, find their passion and know

Reset! A Blueprint for a Better Life

their life purpose almost daily too. My outwardly successful clients will say something like, "I just feel unfulfilled, I have lost my mojo, I know there is something more and it is killing me, but I don't know what it is I want or how to get there". What's more, they are terrified about what they will have to give up if they do tap into it, so it is a real dilemma.

In the next chapter, you will learn my synthesised strategy for a Life Blueprint that moves you from balance to brilliance. It is distilled from nearly three decades of not only working with the world's leading development, spiritual and motivational gurus, but also my life experiences and therapy methods.

For now, let's work on how you can be the person that your dog thinks you are (even if you don't have a dog)!

For starters, make a difference and revisit your 'Stop doing list'. If it isn't on there, add "I will stop talking to myself in such a negative and self-destructive way, which makes every day a soul-sapping experience, lacking in hope and joy". Determining to stop comparing yourself to others. You will either feel better or superior and this may lead to either hubris, being conceited or feeling worse. This may lead to envy, resentment and a feeling of failure on your part.

Social MEdia is so hurtful in this way. It is one of the reasons why so many teenagers (or even children) and young adults feel so depressed and unhappy. To escape those feelings, many turn to self-harming, adopt dysfunctional eating habits, and contemplate – and sadly commit – suicide. When I was a teenager and young adult and I was having a bad day, I'd share my feelings with my diary, listen to something uplifting like Michael Jackson, read something to absorb me and otherwise carry on. When I was a student, the nearest phone was on the corner of the road and you had to have a lot of change in order to share how you were feeling if alone. Now on our mobile phones, or mini computers, we can connect instantly to others in a myriad of ways.

Next, it may be clichéd but it is true that you have to enjoy the journey. Your life is a journey. It is self-evident that the most successful people attain more. If you read any autobiography of a great achiever, you know this to be true. They set goals, as goals are instructions to yourself. When you set a goal, you are commanding yourself and moving in the direction of your vision or dream. Goal setting is the most important skill you can ever develop and it is a skill that is 100% learnable. That's why my first online product, in conjunction with leading business development coach Stuart Ross, is on goal setting (go to goalsetting.training) to enable you to not only follow a proven structure to set goals, but eliminate resistance to them and then embed them at a subconscious level so that they work.

People and organisations with clear visions, values and plans accomplish far more and do it faster than their competitors. In 1979, interviewers asked new graduates from Harvard University's MBA Programme if they had set clear, written goals for their future and made tangible plans to accomplish them.

They discovered that:

84% had no specific goals at all

13% had goals, but they were not committed to paper

3% had clear, written goals and plans to accomplish them

In 1989, the interviewers again interviewed the graduates of that class. They found that the 13% of the class who had goals were earning, on average, twice as much as the 84% who had no goals at all. Even more impressive was that the 3% who had clear, written goals were earning, on average, ten times as much as the other 97% put together.

Self-evidently in life there will never be a straight path from A to Z. The trick is to keep focused on the end game, but be flexible along the way. Curve balls will come your way and you will make mistakes. See your mistakes as invaluable lessons. Learn from them. I used to have a sign next to my desk that said: "I've learnt so much from my mistakes, I think I'll make another." Whilst this is not a life strategy, it is a salient lesson to always remember. If you recall the 'heroic failures' we discussed, you will remember countless examples of this including Einstein who said: "It's not that I am so smart, it's just that I stay with problems longer." He had focus and perseverance.

When you hit bumps in the road, focus on the solution and how to fix it there and then. Just do it. Procrastination is just fear or a need for perfection and neither leads to great results or happy lives. In the novel *La Peste* by Albert Camus, there is a character called Grand who can never complete what he is writing. He must always know more before he can get it right, for example studying Latin, just so he can perfect his French and always find the right word. He has a constant search for knowledge to produce a perfect prose, and because of it his writing lacks heart and is never finished.

Do you think J.K. Rowling works like that? She creates some of the finest and most successful fiction in the world today. She plans meticulously, then sits down each day and puts those words onto paper, and this action together with her amazing imagination brings forth a rich world. If she was still procrastinating about whether Harry should be called Fred, hook up with Hermione, if he has a scar on his forehead or cheek, then millions of children (and adults) around the world would be deprived of the books, movies and theme parks that her genius has spawned.

The director of *Titanic*, *Terminator* and *Avatar*, James Cameron, manages to produce Oscar-winning movies and yet maintain high standards. He says: "People call me a perfectionist, but I'm not. I'm a rightist. I do something until it's right and then I move on to the next thing."

An important next step is to stop comparing yourself to others. By all means 'model' and learn. Model is a more acceptable word for copy. For example, you model your behaviour in a new situation by imitating someone skilled in what you are trying to achieve. Just work out who you want to model. There is an overwhelming array of personal development books with numbers in the title and bespoke frameworks such as *The 7 Habits of Highly Successful People*, *7 Steps to Financial Freedom*, *The 4 Disciplines of Execution*, etc.

Most contain many gems of wisdom and some may be perfect for what you need at that time. This book is a synthesis of some of the principles, universal truths and tried and tested methods that have led to my own insights, therapy practice and life blueprint. Think of it like a car dealership. There are many models. Take some for a test drive, but choose the best one for you to drive around in or you will be back at the bus stop.

Becoming Bulletproof: Whatever advice you try on for size and then walk around with, you must know that fulfilment and success does not come simply because the universe decides life will all go according to your plan. There is no doubt in my mind that you can manifest many wonderful things in your life and that ultimately the universe (or greater force, God, or whatever you choose to call it and believe in) is not 'out to get you'. It actually wants to support you.

As people, jobs, business situations and just about every aspect of your daily life throw up these curve balls, it can feel overwhelming and so many of us feel browbeaten and exhausted by the unrelenting demands of it all. The key is to become bulletproof to it or to see and learn the lessons in adversity.

It is often in what appears to be the greatest moments of challenge that the greatest opportunities and growth arises.

I've been made redundant three times in my life.

The first of my redundancies was in Yorkshire. This wakeup call in my so-called glittering career path led me to think 'What next?' The PR industry was just taking off and I was advised that Lynne Frank's PR was THE agency to work for, so I applied and was called in for an interview where I met Lynne's then husband, Paul Howie. He, like everyone else in the uber trendy glass-ceilinged office, was wearing black and his office resembled a gulag. I sat on a very uncomfortable metal swivel chair on the opposite side of an industrial-sized metal desk. After a while he said: "Well I think we may take you on, but it is up to Lynne, so come next door and meet her." I duly followed and entered what can only be described as a Bedouin tent. Lynne was sitting cross-legged on a Kilim carpet eating macrobiotic food.

Thus I began two years in a world where trips on the Orient Express, breakfast with Daniel Day Lewis, launch events attended by The Rolling Stones and seeing every leading fashion designer in the UK at close quarters were regular occurrences. I cut my teeth on the leading-edge PR of its time, ran an account that was named as one of PR Week's Top Ten Campaigns of the 20th Century (Brylcreem), and put experience on my CV that meant I could walk into my next job, and then start my own highly successful PR agency only a few years later. Thanks redundancy.

My second redundancy came in 1991. The late 80s and early 90s were a crazy time for agency mergers and takeovers and the marketing agency I joined in 1988 was taken over by an advertising agency in 1990 that itself was taken over a year later by Omnicom, which was, at the time, the world's second largest agency group. I was given the choice of either a job at a bigger PR agency that was part of the group or to walk with a redundancy payment. I chose the latter. Setting up shop in my spare bedroom at home, with office furniture bought from a clearance store in East London, my first member of staff was Rosie my Bassett Hound. Husband Mark, thankfully a trained accountant, handled all the finance and frankly anything and everything apart from client work. On day one I had three clients and enough money with their contracts and my £5,000 redundancy package to last the year. Nine years later, having won the coveted PR Week Award for Best Small UK Consultancy and runner-up in the Women into Business Awards, I sold the company when it had a £1.3m turnover.

The third redundancy was a tad unexpected. To be honest, I think they had really wanted to fire me for a while as we were not all seeing eye to eye. What was good was that it was all amicable and I again had time to ask myself, "What now?", and at my first ever foray into online job search I found, and a week later secured, the position as Head of Marketing & Communications at the charity The Leprosy Mission England & Wales. Over five years, amazing work led me to meet some of the world's most disadvantaged and tribal people across Africa and Asia, work with caring co-workers, go on two overseas trips with The Right Hon Ann Widdecombe, spend a lot of time at the House of Lords and enter the world of NGOs, charities and World Health organisations. Redundancy led to the opportunity.

A dear friend of mine, let's call her Lucy, had a financially and emotionally disastrous marriage that necessitated her moving country, struggling as a single mum and starting again. She not only got back on her feet, but started one successful business after another. However, she had a string of unfulfilling love relationships. She was about to 'settle' for a man who really didn't deserve her when she got a speeding fine. In the UK you can mitigate the fine and the endorsement points on your driving licence by attending a Speed Awareness course. Two hours of learning in a classroom environment about the reasons for road rules and regulations. She went along unwillingly, was late, had to sit at the front of the classroom and was told that if she didn't take it seriously, she would be sent out and that the original full fine and penalty points would be incurred. The man next to her laughed and joked with her. They went for a drink afterwards to laugh further. Within a month they were inseparable.

That was four years ago and she is blissfully happy with him. They are moving country and starting a new business together and all because of a speeding fine. You can take your own lesson from this. Perhaps that synchronicity is always there if you let it in. That you can manifest your perfect mate. That even seeming roadblocks and setbacks are often the very way forward. I see all of these in this.

I find I can keep all of this seemingly random synchronicity in mind by visualising a 'Compassion Compass'. Life may seem random, and sometimes our best efforts to plot a course to happiness or fulfilment may get set back or even thwarted, but if you trust that your life is guided by a greater force, in this case, your 'Compassion Compass', then it stops being scary.

A few things led me to establish the 'Compassion Compass'. Compassion is one of the highest values of all, so my vision is of a compass where the set point is firmly in the direction of compassion.

In the early 2000s one of my marketing consultancy clients was True North and I loved the imagery of the True North: the place we all ultimately want to chart our way to. There are many deep and spiritual meanings to the directions of North, South, East and West. Celtic symbolism holds that the East equals air, communication, new beginnings, new growth; South equals fire, energy, passion, creativity; West equals water, emotion, psyche, movement; and North equals earth, home, security and fertility.

With the Compassion Compass the set point is always to be kind to yourself and others. All the strength that you need to save you is within you. The trick is to tap into it, hone it, head towards it, and if the road gets bumpy or you lose your way, trust in your 'Compassion Compass' that maybe things that don't look so good at present are actually there for a good or greater reason. Like my redundancies. Like Lucy's speeding ticket.

It was after studying mindfulness several years ago that I discovered the Gratitude Journals I referred to earlier. Through the expression of gratitude, we are able to not only be present in the moment but by finding the good in even the smallest of things, get flooded with an appreciation that cannot fail to change our mood and outlook for the better. We are always focused on what problems to solve, to the extent that we overwhelm ourselves and put ourselves in a stressed state of constant alert. Think about the word 'overwhelmed'. Then its opposite 'underwhelmed'. We get overwhelmed by the challenges and difficulties of life. We get underwhelmed by ourselves, our responses to life, our visions of the future. Now is the time to change that. Every day there will be something to be grateful for. Even if it was the nice chap on the underground who offered you his seat as he saw how weary you were. A smile from your grandchild. A moment spent watching a bird feed from a tree. Notice and rejoice. By noticing the positive, you start to rewire your brain's neural pathways to think positively on a regular basis. This leads to happiness and happy people release more endorphins, so they are healthier and less stressed. Those who are happy with themselves make better partners in both business and personal lives. They don't need to belittle or control others in order to feel good about themselves. They are able to be at one with themselves and then let others in, and love and support them too.

There are beautiful, soft, leather-bound Gratitude Journals that you can buy, keep by your bed, and work through the exercises they contain every evening and morning. Failing that, you can grab a piece of paper and a pen or use the 'notes' on your computer or phone. Start now. Take a moment and think about, then note down, four things that you are grateful for regarding:

you

your life

your home

your friends/family

Don't be churlish here. You can always find four. Even if you are estranged from your family, perhaps one of the things is that you like the distance! Better still, just be kind and find something, some little nugget of praise or respect that you can offer. If you are not used to using this muscle – the grateful or kind muscle – then think of this as starting with those little weights at the gym. You can work up to the heavy and impressive-looking ones later.

> *"Enjoy the little things, for one day you may look*
> *back and realise they were the big things."*
>
> **Robert Brault**

What you will find, even via this short exercise, is that gratitude works at a feeling, as well as a thinking, level and it makes you more resilient and bulletproof. We speak about 'heartfelt gratitude', not 'intellectual gratitude'. It is a good path to good feelings, and guess who benefits the most when you think about all the things and people you are grateful for? You. Try it without adding yourself to the list. You will still feel better.

Admittedly, there are many challenges. Some workplaces and even home environments can be brutal. Things have come a long way in recent years (certainly in the West) in terms of employee rights and how people expect to be treated in the workplace, but bullying is rife, especially in national institutions, education and healthcare. I know, as many people walk through my door feeling so crushed that they are about to walk away from not just a job but a vocation, and many do. They have months and months off with depression and sickness. It is little consolation that most bullies are weak and were probably bullied themselves. Hurt people hurt people, but when you are the one on the receiving end of the bullying or hurt, especially

Reset! A Blueprint for a Better Life

in a work situation, how do you become bulletproof in order to survive it?

There is a clever technique (or 'hack' as it is now often called) for this, and this short story shared by Marisa Peer perhaps illustrates the best and most effective one of not letting it in.

A journalist goes to interview a holy man and while doing so he rubbishes most of his beliefs and everything he stands for. Throughout the insults and criticisms, the holy man continues to smile, even to beam with happiness and contentment. Finally the journalist says in exasperation: "I don't understand why you are smiling. I have just criticised and mocked you!" The holy man replies: "If you offer me a gift and I do not accept that gift who has it?" "Why, I do," says the journalist. "Exactly," replies the holy man. "I don't accept your criticisms, they belong to you and they can stay with you."

From *Notes from the Universe*:

"Someone bugging you? Nah, way too easy. Just like happiness, disappointment is an 'inside' job."

CHAPTER SEVEN

Create a Compassion Compass and guide your own spiritual life

*"What lies behind us and what lies before us
are tiny matters compared to what lies within us."*

Ralph Waldo Emerson

*"And, when you want something, all the universe conspires
in helping you to achieve it."*

Paulo Coelho, *The Alchemist*

Do these quotes seem contradictory? Well, they are not. They are both on your 'Compassion Compass'. They are the two ends of the tunnel called life. It is about tapping into what is truly inside. Being the best you you can be. Finding your source, your bliss, your inner compass. Then connecting to something greater than you that is right for you and outside of you: your own intuition; The Universe; God; Spirit; Angels; whatever works for you, be it deity or life-force.

"You see, Rosalyn, it was a few gig-a-jillion years ago when I first had my dream. A dream of perfection, imagination and realisation, and because it was my dream, it would inevitably come true and every manifestation would be exactly as it should be. Every detailed part of the plan. Every grain of sand, chiselled long in advance. Nothing would be left to chance, not one second could go astray and not one chuckle. Laugh or cry hadn't been thought of before history's first year.

"So when you realise the degree of attention that was given and you weigh that each blade of grass was considered, dearest, there's only one possible explanation for the image that has become your own.

"You, today, Rosalyn, are exactly who I most wanted to be and being you totally rocks." The Universe

This is an example of the 'Notes from The Universe' that land in my inbox every day via an easy-to-complete free subscription. Written by Mike Dooley, these quirky little nuggets of daily wisdom are also very witty, and due to you having filled in a subscription form with your own personal preferences they always seem just right for you. Spookily so. They certainly seem uncannily accurate about me, my thoughts, my wishes.

For a while, I resisted, as it seemed rather heretical, and then when I started to receive them at a time when I was very low, following the breakdown of my second marriage, I just went with it and felt comforted daily, as if God or The Universe was speaking to me. I then discovered that Mike Dooley is behind the notes, books and retreats, and still managed to hold back my inner cynic that can manifest anytime – a self-appointed guru gives me free advice which invariably leads to a big half-hour webinar (AKA sell) for their online course, book or retreat? As a marketer, I'm all for selling, and as a personal development course attendee veteran, I know that many are really life changing and excellent, but it can be a tiresome model in an overcrowded market. There are sophisticated sales funnels. You get hooked in by an interesting article doing the rounds on Facebook, listen with intent, feel uplifted, and before you know it are reaching for your credit card as that bundle is only $47 if you buy in the time limited window.

Sorting out the wheat from the chaff is key. Isn't it always?

I've looked at Mark Dooley's upsell offerings and they look good. Why wouldn't I want to hook up with some fun, like-minded people and grow and develop? That's why I attend A-Fest. That is why I took the LifeBook course. In the early 90s I had more hunger, which is why Tony Robbins, UPW (Unleash the Power Within), fire walks, fire eating, trapeze jumping and Mastery University filled my quest. When I was in Maui attending Life Mastery, I was reading *The Celestine Prophecy* by James Redfield and *The Way of the Peaceful Warrior* by Dan Millman.

Everyone was buzzing about *The Celestine Prophecy* at that time. It was having a big effect on me as I read it while at Mastery University on the spiritually-charged island of Maui, Hawaii. The day after the course finished, having been hotel-bound for days, my husband and I hired a car and drove to the far side of the island. It is sub-tropical rainforest and really beautiful. There is a series of waterfalls called the Pools of 'Ohe'o (aka Seven Sacred Pools) and we wanted to explore them. We parked in an almost deserted car park after driving through increasingly deserted countryside where we had not seen houses or other people for about an hour before our arrival.

We walked for ages up and up the mountain. It was hot and there was difficult terrain underfoot, with lots of tree roots, jungle creepers and rocks. As we walked, we picked passion fruit and mangoes that were growing wild and were just so happy to be in this beautiful place. Then we came across a man in such a high state of agitation that I thought he was on the verge of a full-fledged panic attack. His teenage son was moodily kicking the ground, eyes cast down, looking utterly despondent. The father explained that they had been up to the waterfalls and were on their way back to the car park. Having stopped to eat some fruit and take a drink, he had realised that his backpack was open and his car keys had dropped out.

He wasn't even sure when and where they had fallen. He did not have a spare set. He said he had been searching fruitlessly for hours. We offered to give him a lift to the nearest town or place to telephone (this was in the days before mobile phones) once we had been up the waterfall and were on our way back down again. We wanted to help, but we had spent hours walking to see these sacred falls and wanted to see it through. For several sweaty hours I'd been imagining jumping into that icy cold water. The man started to calm down a little, but he said that they had to fly out that evening and he didn't know if even this plan would work. I said that it was the only plan, when my husband interjected. To my amazement, he started to tell the man briefly about *The Celestine Prophecy* and manifestation (manifestation means to make public, and can be linked to manifesting an illness in your body on a physical level, and on a spiritual level to making something abstract and thought about real).

My husband asked the sceptical man to describe in detail the car keys. After a churlish, "they are car keys", response, he went along with it. He described them in detail. My husband drilled down: When had he last seen them? Felt them in his rucksack? Can he visualise them in his rucksack. Can he visualise them in the undergrowth?

The man half-heartedly and rather impatiently stood with his eyes closed, 'focusing', when my husband just calmly walked away, not up the mountain, but across to the left, and nearly went out of view. He bent down. He turned round and returned.

He said: "Here they are", and held out his hand with the set of keys in it. Even I was speechless. I'm not sure that the man actually said anything much. I remember he cried and hugged my husband, then me. The boy looked dumbstruck. As they walked away, he shouted: "I'm buying that Celestine book if that is what it can do."

My husband and I finished our trip. As we were driving back in the car, I looked at him and said: "Wow, this takes life to a whole new level, doesn't it?" and it did. When we were pitching for big PR accounts, one for which we were the wildcard on a 10-Way pitch list (meaning that nine top agencies had already been asked to bid and come up with creative ideas for the account and we were added, as a wild outsider, to the process to make it up to 10), we would mock up the front cover of leading trade journal *PR Week* to announce our account win. Copies of this would be posted around the office. I would write out a cheque to my company, RPPR, for the amount of the account and carry it in my purse. I would rehearse stepping on stage to receive my PR Week Award, and in 1999 that is exactly what happened.

Of course we worked hard, gave intelligent and good service, but these visualisations and being open to manifesting always underpinned them. To counter many people who think it is wrong to want things in your life, I believe that if you work towards them and remain open to them then why shouldn't they meet you half way?

When I discovered the cancer, I gave it a name. It was Stephen, as he was a bully at school and had blighted my life at age nine when I had discoloured teeth due to tetracycline staining and was skinny and a swot. I did not have a lump called Invasive Lobular Carcinoma. No, I had a lump called Stephen and every day I would look down at it and say: "I never liked you Stephen. You are a bully. Very soon you will be out of my body and I will never think of you again. Bullies are weak. I'm strong and you will be gone." I was so amazed whilst training to be a therapist to discover that this is an actual technique, to disassociate from something and not own it. "Go me!" I thought. So never speak about 'my cancer'. Speak about 'the cancer' or even better, give it a name of someone you never want to see again.

I shut down my ability to connect at a higher spiritual level for many years and it pained me so much that Citalopram and Zopiclone became my friends. Why did I do this? Well, connecting to the wrong people and being in a work environment that frowned on it, for starters. Having nine major life events in an 18-month period, too. I think even my resilience, hope and faith were dented. The cancer journey had been one of the most spiritual times of my life, but I came back to a 'reduced' world, as a single mother to two challenging children (both adopted as older children and really put into freefall by my illness, the divorce I was going through and two country moves in five years), barely out of cancer treatment and exhausted from radiation, just in time to watch my mother die of pancreatic cancer and try to piece my father's life back together again after his stroke and deep depression. I'd lost my former 'high flying PR guru' status. My large house in London had been sold. The money gone. I turned back to the comfort and rote of my Anglo-Catholic upbringing and this does not entertain the out-there spiritualism I had embraced so actively in the 90s. Truthfully I'd been around spiritual and other-worldly events and experiences all my life.

From childhood I had seen spirits, ghosts and entities. My mother had called me fanciful with a vivid imagination that had

Reset! A Blueprint for a Better Life

helped me to win countless poetry and writing competitions, but I now realise that she had this gift too but didn't like it. Was afraid of it. Shut it down. Countless events happened throughout my childhood and beyond. In my first term of university, I developed severe tonsillitis. No one wanted to look after me as they were all finding out about sex and drugs and rock'n'roll (it was 1980). My parents were too busy running their shop to come and get me. A mature student offered to make me soup, buy Lucozade and get the antibiotics from the chemist. Having no other options, I accepted his help. One day, he produced a glass of water and said he had harnessed the sun's rays in it to heal me. I made him take a sip first. I thought he was about to drug me and do something awful as I lay there feeling vulnerable. Then he said: "Why do you fear it so and shut it down?" I knew immediately what he was speaking about. I told him about all my childhood experiences and he just kept nodding.

I can't remember the rest of the conversation or him really. Once I was better I embraced student life with the same gusto as the rest. Occasionally I even read the course books and went to lectures.

Throughout my 20s, a few very significant happenings and sightings occurred, but they started to scare me so the shutdown came more. It was only in my 40s that one day it kicked back with such a force and certainly that I was able to actually pursue a course of legal action against someone as I had total certainty that I had been wronged and I was proved right. In the High Court.

So this 'gift' has flip-flopped for years. Now I'm embracing it again. Visualisations are back. I have my mood board in front of me as I write this now. My picture above me reads: 'Your Thoughts Become Things'. This embraces the rule of the mind that your brain can't differentiate between what you imagine and what really is. That is why people have stress-related illnesses from worry. They are 'visualising' something terrible happening and their mind holds onto this image and their body has a physical response to it. I started the day, as I aim to start every day, with a meditation. I became open to opportunities and didn't try to force them, and in a short period of time I was offered a radio show, a newspaper column, two new business ventures, and my therapy clients just grew and grew with new appointment requests dropping into my inbox every day.

I unblocked my relationship corner and am manifesting my perfect partner, although daring to be vulnerable in this online dating world can really hurt at times.

This is all underpinned with hard work, my marketing expertise, a lot of networking, much study and a rather large dose of what we call in the UK nous (common sense or trusting your inner wisdom).

Recently, I've come across some arguments and discussions that basically rubbish most of those who offer advice or courses based on *The Secret* or *The Laws of Abundance*. Perhaps there is a secret behind *The Secret?* I don't know but I do know that when I work on myself, fill myself with as much positivity as I can muster, create vision boards, clear intention lists and goals, am grateful every day and see everything, even the curved balls, as a possible opportunity, then life just gets better and better. I don't like the habit of denigrating our idols or things to be believed in. As Gustav Flaubert says in one of my all-time favourite books, *Madame Bovary*: "The denigration of those we love always detaches us from them in some degree. Never touch your idols, the gilding will stick to your fingers."

And underpinning it all I remember to enjoy the journey and have fun.

My spiritual and non-spiritual friends alike say things like: "You are a different person to a few years ago. It is like you have shed a skin. A butterfly emerging from a chrysalis." These are so much better to hear that the sorts of things I was hearing when I was at odds with myself. Damaging things like: "Why can't you just be like everyone else, like normal people?", "Why can't you just do it this way, the right way?", "I just don't get how your mind works? How did you come up with that?"

I remember sitting on a plane, looking out the window as we climbed above the clouds. A deep sorrow filled me. "I'm in the wrong life", I realised. "But I don't know how to get out of it." That was then. Now, using all the tools I share in this book, I do. It's been one heck of a journey but at least I can share it with you now.

A couple of things that always saw me true were sayings from my mum and myself. My mum would always say: "To thine own self, be true." I held onto that, even when I wasn't sure who I was, or at times of disease or depression, as I knew I was not living a life that was aligned with my true values or true self.

As a teenager I ran, as part of a Sixth Form project, a Young Enterprise company. We made some truly terrible wooden mahjong boards that no one knew how to play and sold plaster cast DIY Garden Gnome kits where you made from home-mixed plaster of Paris your own small garden ornament (sadly at a time when they had not become kitsch). When we made our public presentation about how well our Young Enterprise company had done (a bit like in *The Apprentice* when they are in the boardroom and the sales figures are in), I was asked at the end of it all what I had learned and what this would mean my future Life Mantra was. I said that what I'd learned was that: "Life is full of endless possibilities". It has stood me in good stead, even if at the time it was awful trying to sound wise when we had failed to sell hardly any of our products.

At Mastery University we went through a 'what would people say at your funeral eulogy?' exercise. This is very sobering. You get to hover above the service and hear what is being said about you. You then get to decide what would be a wonderful thing to hear. Being poetic and loving a rhyme I came up with 'Rosalyn was a life shaker, soul waker and money maker'. It seems to have come true.

A good question to ask yourself is: "If I could be remembered for one thing, what would that be?" "If I had an inscription on my tombstone, what would it say?" This really helps you focus on your life purpose. Why not take 10 minutes now. Put the book down and think this through, then jot down what comes to mind. Look at it often. Does it ring true? Does it serve you well? Is this as good as it gets? There is still time to write a new future, a new eulogy. Start now.

So what other life-giving concepts are good to embrace, try on like a new pair of shoes, walk around in for a while and see if they are comfortable for you too?

Things such as calling on angels and spiritual guides, although I've been told by several people that I have a very strong spirit guide and a bunch of angels looking out for me. This must be true, as I've come back from life-threatening illnesses and situations at least five times.

Energy clearing is good. We had the office Feng Shui'd in the 90s, even featuring on the front cover of the Feng Shui magazine. By opening the energy of the office and adding water features (and things like salt in certain places), the aim was to make it a better, more energised, healthier place to be. It worked. Sickness levels and absenteeism dropped significantly in the following months and we all anecdotally felt it a nicer, more open place to be.

Discovering your hidden health secrets or listening to your body to enable you to eat right is now gathering momentum. In the 90s, I would sit at the table and, before taking the menu, ask my body what it wanted to eat. It would answer. 'Fish today' or 'salad' or whatever. It knew. Interestingly I avoided carbs for years (Atkins was all the rage), but following the radiation treatment I became the Carb Queen overnight. The Olive Garden restaurant situated close to the Moffitt Cancer Clinic in Tampa was like a magnet to my seven-stone vegan body. When one day I drank two cokes from a vending machine (to flush out the residue of the radioactive barium drink I'd had prior to a CT scan) and then said I had to go to Olive Garden and ate a huge plate of pasta with a side of garlic bread, I think my husband thought I'd lost it. I later discovered that the body needs plenty of energy to sustain itself through radiation treatment and that healthy carbs are a good choice. Refined carbs such as the ones I craved for a few days are not so good as they can cause the blood sugar levels to spike, but once my week-long brachytherapy radiation treatment was over we were back on the airplane to our organic farm where I lived on the land and sea with natural foods and liquids for a year while my body recovered.

So you need to not only listen to your body, but also understand the best way of answering it.

Other useful methodologies include the psychology of states of being that include mindfulness (being very present in the moment and calming your body and mind), rapid transformational therapy (freeing people from patterns of behaviour by uncovering and healing past hurts and traumas), ecopsychology practices (drawing on the deep bond between humans and nature), spirituality (connecting to a higher self or being), traditional religions and prayer, neuroscience (study of the nervous system), neurobiology (the cells of the nervous system), shamanism (based on ancient teachings about the connection of nature and mankind), expanded states of consciousness (the third eye in yoga practices or hallucinogenic states as per those induced by drugs where you enter another worldly state either within your body or external to it), chakra balancing (as understood in many medicines, such as acupuncture, there are seven main energy centres in the body, known as chakras that correlate to specific body ailment and physical dysfunctions. Balancing the chakras can balance one's physical and emotional state), tantra (born from the ancient esoteric traditions of Hinduism and Buddhism, this mainly relates to a form of intimacy between people that connects them at a mind and body level), planetary forces (think of the 'Blue Moon' when people said they went crazy or just a full moon that can influence tides and certainly animals), past life regressions (where you are taken, via a trance-like state, to recall past lives often to unlock patterns or pains in present ones) and no doubt many tools I have not even discovered. I'm sure that if I went to an event such as Burning Man I would be in a state of perpetual discovery!

One thing is for sure. The world has come a long way since the days when I thought that a fire walk was the most amazing paradigm shift imaginable! Tony Robbins and Unleash the Power Within weekend is all about the fire walk. You end up taking off your shoes and socks and walking calmly over burning hot coals to prove that you no longer have limiting beliefs. It is a metaphor. If you can decide that this fire walk won't burn you, then what can life throw at you that you can't cope with? Having done several fire walks I can attest that it is a powerful experience.

In recent years my 'cannot live without' action is yoga. I've been on several yoga retreats where it becomes a lifestyle practice, healing and strengthening your body not only through the yoga, but also through eating the right diet, breathing, meditating, using herbs to balance the body, and visualising, aligning your energy to natural ones, and really remembering that your thoughts become things and who you are on the inside governs who you are on the outside in terms of how you navigate through life. I see it as a self-hypnosis for the body, mind and soul.

The yoga practice itself is designed to create strength (starting with your core, inner strength and alignment) and harmony in both the mind and body. I've practiced several types including Kundalini, Ashtanga, Hatha and Iyengar. I see merits in them all and actually like to shake them up a bit and cross from one 'school' to another from time to time. Some have a more rapid and fluid flow, others focus on ritualised postures that are held for longer, still others focus on breathing or being centred. All include stretching, posture and balance work. Contrary to popular belief, you don't have to be super bendy. I'm not and I've been practicing on and off for over 20 years.

What I do know is that benefits include reduction of pain and stiffness, better flexibility, improved sleep and the ability to relax, muscles that are stronger and more toned, better breathing, more energy and quicker recovery from injury. When I attended a five-day yoga retreat in Spain recently I was wearing my Bellabeat Fitness Tracker that measures, among other things, your stress levels. Mine are usually around the 35% mark on an average day. Arriving with a 28% reading, I was amazed, after the five days, to see that it had dropped to 6%. Proof indeed of the benefits of yoga (and a vegan diet, no alcohol, sunshine, walks and a good night's sleep!

One day Alice came to a fork in the road and saw a Cheshire cat in a tree. "Which road do I take?" she asked. "Where do you want to go?" was his response. "I don't know," Alice responded. "Then," said the cat, "it doesn't matter."

Lewis Carroll

I see many clients whose feelings range from a sense of general malaise: there is something missing in their life, right through to those who are consumed with self-loathing and feel like utter failures. On more than one occasion I have been told that they "just take up oxygen that could be being used by someone better", or really think that the world would be a better place if they were no longer in it. There is a host of complex reasons as to what may have triggered these feelings or led them into behaviours that they now regret or into living compromised lives, but when I ask the question: "How would you like to feel?" they may answer: "Happy, light, at ease in my own skin, filled with self-love, wanting to get up every day".

When I ask: "What would your life look like in order to have these things?" or "Where do you need to head in order to get them?" the inevitable answer is: "That is the problem. I just don't know. I know I should follow my dream but I don't know what it is. I so want it, but I can't get it as I have no idea what it looks like, or if I have an idea I just think I'll screw up on the way to get it or that it will take too long to get my ducks in line to even attempt to go there. I look back at my life that led to this point and I feel such a failure."

Reset! A Blueprint for a Better Life

I had one client who, when I was discussing how we could make her handle the next 40 or so years of her life in a happier healthier way, said that the prospect of even one more year was more than she could bear to think about. Yet she had travelled a great distance to see me. To find the release and the joy she thought almost impossible.

Given that you have to start from where you are, the first step is to take a snapshot of your present situation across six key areas of your life. I often use a quick version of this exercise, using only five areas as it is so easy to remember. Stretch out one hand and look at your fingers. You have five and you have five key areas of your life that are all necessary, just like five fingers are necessary to a fully-functioning hand for balance and key performance.

The key areas are: Faith, Fitness, Friends, Family and Finance.

The sixth F is one that I've added recently as I need to remind myself to have more of it: Fun!

There is a seventh F which I don't include on the framework or have clients score as it is rather difficult to assign a number to it and it can ebb and flow. It is a category I've found one of the hardest to master in my life and yet it is a key component to getting your joy back. It is Forgiveness.

I'm a visual learner so I find that having an easy to see visual of this mapped out is really useful. When visited on a quarterly basis, you can easily compare the latest one with ones you mapped in previous quarters and see immediately where progress has and has not been made. In an easy-to-use spider diagram you can plot out across a number of axes where you are in terms of Good-Bad on each of the six categories.

The link to your own diagram is at the end of this book. Click on it, and a download and full instructions for the exercise are available.

Here is a story that I have heard many times over the last 20 years and is a gentle reminder to not get caught up in the belief that there is too much to handle and that 24 hours in a day are not enough. It always makes me smile:

The Mayonnaise Jar and Two Cups of Coffee

A professor stood before his philosophy class and had some items in front of him. When the class began, he wordlessly picked up a very large and empty mayonnaise jar and proceeded to fill it with golf balls. He then asked the students if the jar was full. They agreed that it was.

The professor then picked up a box of pebbles and poured them into the jar. He shook the jar lightly. The pebbles rolled into the open areas between the golf balls. He then asked the students again if the jar was full. They agreed it was.

The professor next picked up a box of sand and poured it into the jar. Of course, the sand filled up every space that was left. He asked once more if the jar was full. The students responded with a unanimous "yes".

The professor then produced two cups of coffee from under the table and poured the entire contents into the jar effectively filling the empty space between the sand. The students laughed.

"Now," said the professor as the laughter subsided, "I want you to recognise that this jar represents your life. The golf balls are the important things – your

family, your children, your health, your friends and your favourite passions – and if everything else was lost and only they remained, your life would still be full.

The pebbles are the other things that matter, like your job, your house and your car.

The sand is everything else – the small stuff. "If you put the sand into the jar first," he continued, "there is no room for the pebbles or the golf balls. The same goes for life. If you spend all your time and energy on the small stuff you will never have room for the things that are important to you.

"Pay attention to the things that are critical to your happiness. Play with your children. Take time to get medical checkups. Take your spouse out to dinner. Play another 18. There will always be time to clean the house and fix the disposal. Take care of the golf balls first – the things that really matter. Set your priorities. The rest is just sand."

One of the students raised her hand and inquired what the coffee represented. The professor smiled. "I'm glad you asked.

"It just goes to show you that no matter how full your life may seem, there's always room for a couple of cups of coffee with a friend."

So go ahead and print out and map your first 6 Fs Framework now.

CHAPTER EIGHT

Tapping into your Personal Power via the 6 Fs

The last three or four 'reps' are crucial to making a muscle grow. This area of endurance (sometimes pain) divides the champion from someone who is not a champion. It's what most people lack, having the guts to go on and say they'll go through the pain no matter what happens, or being crazy and masochistic enough. It depends on your viewpoint. What is not in doubt is that many people who really win, especially in the fields of sport, do so because of this unrelenting resolve.

You don't get to have Beyoncé's bootylicious bottom just by watching her jiggle it a lot on MTV videos. You do have to do some 'heavy lifting' yourself. However, I'm not going to take you through a 'no pain no gain' plan as via the page **www.resetyourjoy.com** you can access a transformational hypnotherapy exercise that will allow you to be open to the changes you want and to embed them into your life. After all, it is a blueprint for your journey.

Before you listen to it you must find a quiet place where you won't be disturbed, and read the terms and instructions for a safe and relaxing hypnotherapy session on the page www.resetyourjoy.com

What is common to all the categories across the Formula 6 Framework is being clear about where you are headed and what you want to change. In other words, being clear about goals, as evidence shows that successful people are goal oriented and clear about the process. They anticipate what resources they will need along the way, what possible obstacles they may meet and need to prepare for, who they need to tell and involve and ask favours of, and what they need to stop doing in order to make it a success. They go beyond using SMART goals. They evaluate what the ticket for this journey will cost them and dare to ask themselves if they are willing to pay this price and determine how strong their resolve is to make this happen.

They have 'must', not 'should'. Tony Robbins broke any attachment to the word 'should' that I may have had in the early 90s. He said repeatedly that people 'Shoulded all over themselves' in such a way as to make it sound like 'shitted'. I hear it all the time from people. They ask me something like, "Tell me about how you changed career as I want to do that?" I answer, in detail. "Oh yes", comes the reply, "I should do that." Guess what? You won't until it's a must. Until it is a must in your life and you can't think of not doing it. Until you are so excited about how achieving this goal and the life or rewards it will bring becomes a living vision for you. It becomes part of 'brand you'. Again, make it compelling. It is the difference between "I should get up early every day to exercise as it is good for me" vs "I must get up early every day to choose exercise as my way to start my day so I start with a win, lose half a stone and look amazing on the beach this summer".

Reset! A Blueprint for a Better Life

Having a narrow focus is also a proven strategy for success, but this needs to come with flexibility and the ability to adapt and be open to change when necessary. Watching the excellent movie *Dunkirk* directed by Christopher Nolan reinforced this for me. I love the intensity of the early scenes of this movie and understood so much more about the historic event. It is a perfect example of 'have a single purpose' and 'be flexible to re-evaluate if this can't be met'. At first the objective is: 'Hold the knoll'. When they are driven back from this it is: 'Ensure we protect the jetty so that the large boats can evacuate the troops'. When the jetty is blown up it is: 'Build a temporary jetty and ask for help'. The men who are saved leave via this temporary jetty but mostly via the rescue fleet of every available boat from the English coast which brings that help.

© Rosalyn Palmer

Further Fs in detail

Many of the Fs have been examined in detail in earlier chapters. However, some bear further scrutiny and explanation.

1. Fitness

Throughout my life there have been only a few sustained times when I was both fit and healthy. I've pretty much been on a quest for optimal health since my mid 20s and that is why I'm able to share this book with you today. Without the steps I've taken and continue to take every day, I simply don't think I would be here.

I now realise how important 'food as medicine' has been throughout my life. When I was 18 months old, my lungs collapsed due to misdiagnosed whooping cough and German measles. I was pumped full of antibiotics and for good measure was prescribed them regularly throughout my entire childhood. A childhood that was often spent in bed, as whatever virus or infection was doing the rounds would hone in on my compromised immune system.

Yet when I was well, I was full of energy and loved to do gymnastics, climb trees, ride my bike and do outdoors things. I loved camping with the Girl Guides, and The Duke of Edinburgh Awards would see me traipsing across wet stretches of Derbyshire or Yorkshire, backpack on. I think the thing that sustained me throughout these years was the best medicine available: fresh food. I am a grocer's daughter and lived above the shop until I was five. My grandmother, who was one of 14 siblings, lived with us until I was 11. She, and her sister Emma, made 'proper food': homemade pies, roasts and bakes, accompanied by lots of vegetables.

I'm also thankful that in my 20s, when I was working long hours at Lynne Franks PR, I discovered, as they were then referred to, complementary medicines and practices. Partying too hard and probably drinking too much, my immune system rebelled and I was pill popping to get past the IBS, allergies, psoriasis, lack of periods and constant bouts of tonsillitis. My hormones were a mess. Thankfully many of the staff at Lynne Franks PR were Buddhists and people who, even in the late 80s, were very aware of healthy whole food, complementary medicine and therapies. So I embraced acupuncture, meditation, *The Cranks Vegetarian Cookbook*, well-chosen supplements, colonics and Kinesiology.

Learning about optimal health is very very confusing and often challenging, with lots of seemingly contradictory information. I became a vegetarian in the early 90s thinking it a better and healthier choice for my body and digestive system, but not knowing any better, I made up for my lack of 'protein' through a lot of dairy, so it was fortunate that my next step in the path of good health came when I attended Health Mastery and my understanding about diet, nutrition and fitness increased exponentially.

I was trying to get pregnant at the time. I should have known that 'trying' was a poor choice and that my body was not able to really grow and nurture another human at that time. Despite all the good things I was doing, I was working 80-hour weeks, highly stressed, sleeping badly, drinking too much and pretty depleted. Every day I'd juice and down cod liver oil and folic acid. Each week I'd visit the acupuncture clinic, and a wonderful masseuse called Kim would come to my house to give me a relaxing Swedish massage. We even had a sitting massage chair in the office and offered lunchtime distress massages that I loved, along with going to yoga. I had colonics at the Hale Clinic, and seeing the contents of my colon as they bobbed along the transparent tube next to me led me to cut down substantially on dairy, realising how mucus-forming it was.

So I dug deeper into the mind and body connection. I went on retreats, embraced a deep mind/body/cellular healing process called The Journey, developed by my former PR client Brandon Bays, and saw an amazing Ayurvedic doctor. As time passed and I still was not conceiving, I was referred to more and more experts, including healer Jack Temple who would strap tablets onto my body and have me sit in his stone circle (henge) to draw out the toxins from my body. I signed up for floatation tanks. After one, I sobbed uncontrollably for several hours. It was cathartic and I was hopeful. My food choices became ever more selective, especially as I'd put on some weight (from all the meals out I was eating for my role as MD of a PR company). I took a one-day per week membership to the Sanctuary Spa in Covent Garden and blocked out every Wednesday afternoon. I would be driven to that Spa and it literally was my sanctuary.

After two years, always believing I'd found the silver bullet of good health at each new turn, and yet still not pregnant, I finally went to the doctor. He immediately sent my husband and me for all the tests possible including a laparoscopy for me and rooms with embarrassing porno magazines for my husband. Nothing was found. Non-specific infertility. So very frustrating, as there was nothing to 'cure'. We were offered IVF, but turned it down. It just seemed so invasive and unnatural to us at the time. We decided to adopt instead, and thus started 18 months of a new kind of intrusion as we were vetted within an inch of our lives.

If only I'd known then what I know now. That the one thing stopping me from getting pregnant was my mind. It was protecting me from burdening my body further, and also there was ambiguity in my mind as I would worry about how we could possibly care for a baby as the demands of the business seemed so unrelenting.

Reset! A Blueprint for a Better Life

I'd probably got close to conceiving when I was struck down with Dengue Fever. Both my husband and I caught it in the Bahamas, but as he showed the symptoms first he was admitted to a nice private hospital courtesy of PPP. I, instead, was at home, as our adopted son was now with us and I couldn't leave him.

Over a seven-week period I lost 26 pounds. At this, I was delighted. The size zero model look was all the rage and now at under seven stone (98lbs/44.45kg) I was pretty much a size zero. I loved it, and coupled with several years of having a personal trainer, I was suddenly, in my mind, 'super fit'.

What I had done had turned my obsessive energy about the business into being obsessed about my body.

My Ayurvedic doctor had asked me a year earlier if I thought the mental or the physical breakdown would win and I'd laughed and told him of all the 'good' healthy things I was doing. He had shaken his head and said in his soft voice: "We are just sticking plasters on your life. You have to address that life and change it. Soon." He told me several years later that he had seen the cancer marker in my eye two years before it manifested. I asked him why he hadn't warned me and he said that the cancer may never have developed so why put me into a mindset to trigger it. This I now totally hold to be true.

The cancer journey has been the most intense of all my health journeys. It was also the most life-affirming and spiritually uplifting.

My diagnosis came on the day before Good Friday. I was 43 years old. I was living in Nassau where you have to have private medical healthcare. We had a good private policy which gave me a once-a-year 'well woman' check. In February I had a mammogram and had been given the all clear, but almost immediately afterwards, whilst in the shower, I found a lump in my right breast. Because I'd had the all clear from the mammogram I waited for a few weeks and then still feeling this hard round lump, I presented myself to Dr Van Tooren, my wonderful GP. He wasn't happy and booked me into hospital the next day for an ultrasound. Although I was feeling in very good health on the whole, with hindsight I realise that my immune system was running down. I was super-fit and still running that 5 km every morning prior to the gym, but since January I'd noticed that I was having to break my run with intermittent walking as I was tired.

Even when I went for the ultrasound, I was thinking it was probably just a cyst, but Bahamians are quite emotional, and after the procedure the nurse grabbed my hand and said: "Live every day as if it's your last!" It hit me like a freight train and I said to myself: "Oh God, is this something serious then?" I hadn't even taken anyone to hospital with me. They asked me to come in the next day for a large needle biopsy. My husband accompanied me this time and four days later, sitting in Dr Van Tooren's surgery, he quietly told me that it was cancer. A particularly fast-growing and invasive form of breast cancer.

The next day we went away, as already planned, on holiday to the out island of Eleuthera. I can remember the alarm going off and getting the boys ready, driving to the ferry and standing on the deck of the Sea Wind ferry as it pulled out of Nassau Harbour, feeling like I was leaving all life behind. As I pulled away and withdrew, the kids needed even more attention and it was pretty brutal. I had to get out of the car on the long drive from The Current to Tarpum Bay, stand by the side of the deserted landscape and scream. This scared everyone.

Given the type of cancer and the age of our kids, we then had to return to Nassau after a few days and be really practical and consider our options quickly. I chose the Moffitt Cancer Center in Tampa, not just for its outstanding reputation but also because the Moffitt is an independent clinic and I felt that some of the other hospitals were in the pockets of the pharmaceutical companies and were bound to suggest a very oncological course of treatment. As I was into very holistic health, I wanted to know that I was going somewhere where they would listen to me and I could make good choices, rather than having some chemotherapy-focused regime.

Three weeks later I was on the operating table. My initial diagnosis of invasive lobular carcinoma was not good. My doctor had advised a double mastectomy and the Moffitt carried out further tests. They have one of the most advanced breast MRI machines in the world and found five lumps, in addition to the one confirmed as cancer, across both breasts. They recommended a double mastectomy, chemotherapy and radiation treatment. Because of my young kids, I had an appointment with the plastic surgeon straight away. The operation was booked in for the following week.

It was Sunday and we found a local church to go to in Tampa, and while the service was mid-way, I fainted. I later found out that all the people in my home New Providence Community Church I had attended in the Bahamas had been praying for me at that very time. I came out of the church and had a feeling of total certainty that all the other lumps were not cancerous. Early Monday morning I rang the hospital, spoke to my amazing surgeon Dr Cox and told him how I felt. He said to come straight in, and after further discussions, he said that they would biopsy each new lump the following day, one after the other. He said that if all five were not positive, then I would have defied all odds and all of their best assessments of the new tests.

I did defy the odds. I had five biopsies, one after the other. As each one was taken, it was sent to the lab, we waited and then the results came back. Negative. So onto the next one. Negative and on to the next one and the next and the next. By this time, I had so much Lidocaine pumped into me that two interns were holding me down on the table for the last biopsy. I didn't care. It came back negative. Dr. Cox came to the room and told me that the Brits are made of strong stuff and gave me a hug. I had a lumpectomy that week and flew home.

Two weeks later I returned for brachytherapy radiation. It is a newer (especially 13 years ago) form of radiation that cuts down the time from five weeks to five days by delivering a higher dose of radiation to a smaller area of the breast. Mine was MammoSite or Balloon internal radiation.

I chose the treatment and I know that they gave me the best option. Sadly I know now that I wasn't perhaps the best candidate as my breasts were small and this led to complications that I still have today including fat necrosis, scarring, breast pain, spasms under my arms and aching ribs, but I'm here and we made the best decisions we could at the time.

And at the time this treatment also knocked me for six. Thankfully we had made another good choice: to allow time for nature to heal a body that science had saved.

Following a chance conversation at a party with Ian Goodfellow of Goodfellows Farm, shortly before all the treatment happened, we discovered that he was keen to rent out his 10-acre farm in Eleuthera. What better place to recover than an organic farm

Reset! A Blueprint for a Better Life

that fronted one of the most beautiful pink sand beaches in the world?

We moved there. For two years we lived on the land and sea. I would haggle daily with the local fishermen for their catches of grouper, snapper, hogfish, shark or lobster. I'd added fish to my otherwise vegan diet. The farm was abundant with fruits. We grew mixed salad greens and watercress and I moved onto aubergines, courgettes, carrots and onions. I purchased bushels (large cardboard boxes) of amazing mangoes from Mr Pinder from Spanish Wells (an island at the top of Eleuthera). I swapped homemade onion bread for tuna. I distilled Noni juice.

I meditated, read, watched positive movies and walked the beach with my dogs. The cats would follow us twice a day down the path and stop just before the sand dunes and wait so that when I returned I would have an entourage of three dogs and two cats behind me. I'd swim in the sea, with my dog Tarpum swimming at my side. First to one palm tree and then back. Then two and eventually to the length of the beach and back, always keeping an eye out for the many sharks, stingrays and barracudas.

It was one of the most amazing and uplifting times of my life and I recovered fully.

But the challenges continued.
Strong trees do not grow with ease
The stronger the wind
The stronger the trees.

Like that poem, I now see all the adversity was there for a reason, to make me stronger or to make me stop and listen to my body and to my inner wisdom or to see the bigger picture. It was actually easier when it was my own health journey to do this. When it was happening to those I love it was more difficult. My father was still recovering from his stroke in the UK and very depressed. That was why my mother had been unable to come over to be with me.

We were hit with two hurricanes, and in the second one lost all of the fruit and pretty much all we were growing apart from the watercress that loved the extra water.

Six months after my diagnosis my mother was diagnosed with terminal pancreatic cancer. Immediately after our phone lines had been reinstated following the hurricane I had a very troubling conversation with her when she said she had jaundice and had been for tests for a 'stomach problem'. My instinct told me it was much worse, so despite the chaos at the farm, my schedule of follow-up hospital appointments, the kids who were in a sort of freefall and a very withdrawn husband, I flew back to the UK and sat in the Queen's Medical Centre with my sister and mother to hear that she had terminal pancreatic cancer and an estimated six months to live.

I spent two years visiting hospitals for my treatment or to see my father or support my mother. It changed everything in my life. It stripped away everything I had had or known from me.

Of the decisions we made then (and hindsight would make me take a different choice) the sale of our London home at a time when I couldn't really make a good decision, probably hurt the most. My husband had also made several poor financial investments, and when I found out about the financial losses, plus many other personal issues, it was the tipping point. I was sadly unable to continue in my marriage or living overseas. I returned to the UK as a jobless, homeless, single mother in time

Reset! A Blueprint for a Better Life

to watch my mother die. In time to go through a gruelling court case accused of child abduction under The Hague Convention. In time to Reset! Again.

I had been given a book by the church counsellor when I discovered the cancer called *Pain, The Gift No One Wants*. It is about leprosy. The charity I worked for is The Leprosy Mission. Synchronicity.

Even at the darkest of times, I felt that everything including the cancer was for a reason. The cancer woke me up to my spiritual calling. It changed everything and after charity marketing and sadly a second marriage (to my childhood sweetheart) that ended in divorce, I was approached by Marisa Peer to train in her inaugural intake of therapists. Now I help to train others, and I help people and change lives and even, according to the feedback I get, save lives. I combine my extensive training, ongoing thirst for knowledge and constant improvement. Who would have known that there are so many transferable skills from PR and marketing to hypnotherapy? The ability to communicate, create rapport, understand people quickly and get to the nub of an issue. Most importantly I bring empathy and compassion. I've probably been there and not only survived but thrived. Cancer gave me this gift. It is a gift. I thank it. I was also angry that it took my mother from me. What I know is that everyone's cancer journey is their own. Mine is positive.

I learned how to stop ageing from Marisa Peer who can command the brain and thus the body's cells to slow down the ageing process through RTT. It was fascinating to learn how to tap into your spiritual guides and sense of spiritual self from Sonia Choquette (whose exercise is included earlier in this book), and to understand the difference between guided meditations, mindfulness and true meditation from Emily Fletcher of Ziva meditation, and be reminded of the detrimental health effects of sugar from JJ Virgin.

My skin was never so clear and glowing as after a week of drinking nothing but juice, so another quick hack to remember is drink or eat something green every day. Drink lots of water. Start each day with lemon juice (and fresh ginger in winter or if you have a cold) in very warm water to flush out the toxins from the body that need releasing. I then have a tablespoon of organic apple cider vinegar in water and take a high strain probiotic before breakfast. Years of antibiotics plus other medicines and medical treatments left me with a 'leaky gut', so by creating an alkaline environment with the vinegar and then giving my gut added healthy bacteria I am able to better digest and absorb the good food I put in each day. In turn this leads to a healthy immune system and a healthy nervous system. It is also a way to stave off food intolerances that can lead to other health issues too, including fatigue and depression.

What does my diet look like now? Well, it is still evolving. Having suffered from IBS on and off for decades I have a FODMAP app on my phone and choose what food and drinks I consume carefully if I'm having a flare up. FODMAPs are a collection of carbohydrates and sugar alcohols found in food and drinks. When consumed FODMAPs can be poorly absorbed in the small intestine and pass through to the large intestine, where they are readily fermented by bacteria in the large bowel, contributing to the production of gas. FODMAPs are also highly osmotic, meaning that they attract water into the large bowel, which can alter how quickly the bowels move. These two processes can then trigger symptoms including excess wind, abdominal bloating and distension, abdominal pain, constipation or diarrhoea, or a combination of both.

Reset! A Blueprint for a Better Life

What I do understand is how the most common dis-ease and ill-health conditions are caused by inflammation, so decreasing it in your body is key and that it starts with the gut. My good friend Linda Booth, AKA The Tummy Queen, is an expert in this respect so do sign up for her Facebook page Tummy Talk, where she not only gives wonderful free advice but will also answer your queries as she is on a mission to help heal all our tummies.

I've recently tried intermittent fasting which has a whole body of evidence regarding its efficacy. It is actually easy. You just have to go 14 hours without eating. So if you get an early night, say 9pm you can eat again at midday the next day. It is not a great hardship. I will also only drink lemon water and herb teas up to this time. I do it once a week. The benefits of intermittent fasting include the body inducing important cellular repair, changing for the better genes related to longevity, increase in the blood levels of the human growth hormone that facilitates fat burning and muscle gain, plus meaning that less calories are consumed and more are burnt due to increased metabolic rate during the 'fast' period leading to potential weight loss.

I've also detoxed via an Adrenal Rest diet. It really worked and was not hard to follow. I went from three back-to-back prescriptions for antibiotics for a persistent chest infection to feeling great. The reset diet allowed me to rebuild the integrity of my whole body from the inside out.

I do juice, but not all the time. After three trips to Jason Vales' Juicy Oasis, I feel I know when to dip in and out of juicing and often I prefer some roughage in my food so I will use my Nutribullet for a smoothie instead. I eat lots of vegetables and a small selection of fruit (many fruits are not IBS gut friendly and you must also remember that a lot of fruit has natural fruit sugar so eat it in moderation). With the FODMAP app on my phone, I can easily navigate all this and I try to stick to it as much as I can with the exception of avocados as I love them, and now I'm following the Ketogenic diet I want those essential fats. Speaking of which, my new favourite cookbook is *Fat for Fuel (A revolutionary diet to combat cancer, boost brain power and increase your energy)* by Dr Joseph Mercola. He aims to address a defective metabolism that is a result of mitochondrial dysfunction through high fat foods. All I can say to its claims is that I love the recipes, they include most of the foods I would eat naturally and I feel better and am sleeping much better too.

I have tea and oat or almond milk (I've moved away from soya due to things I've read and personal taste preferences) and lots of herbal teas. Also my friend Linda's Tummy Tea.

While I have come very close to being vegan (being a pescatarian for years) I do now eat some meat (organic chicken and the odd rib eye steak) and fish.

I eat mindfully, chew a lot and don't drink water until at least 10 minutes after the meal, unless I'm in a restaurant or at a dinner party when you tend to eat and drink at the same time.

In addition to yoga, meditation, Zumba, walks in nature and the odd bike ride, the one thing that I'm now super-focused on is having an amazing sex life. I want my body to be flooded with endorphins on a regular basis, and orgasms are something I didn't really have for years. I was good at faking, as a way of getting the man to ejaculate and make it end quickly, even in my marriages when I was tired and stressed.

When I went back to dating in my 50s, I thought that perhaps this was a forbidden territory for me. That I should settle for nice cuddles, easy sex, companionship and someone to grow old with and end times of loneliness.

Attending A-Fest, working with Marisa Peer and Ester Perel and discovering Tantra put paid to that. I now LOVE orgasms, can have multiple and full body ones and increasingly they involve other people and not just my vibrator or me alone. The good thing is that I understand my body and its responses better than ever before, so I'm able to share that knowledge.

Once my mind bought into the physical and emotional benefits of orgasms, they just started to happen.

Orgasms:

Are nature's way of improving fertility by stimulating your hypothalamus gland to release reproductive hormones that induce ovulation and cervical fluid. They are nature's green light and even after our fertile years we don't have to go to amber and red.

Are nature's way of regulating our hormonal cycle by improving circulation to organs in the pelvic cavity. Again they are nature's green light.

Provide lymphatic drainage, helping the body to detoxify, improve digestion and mood and prevent disease.

Fight heart disease and osteoporosis by promoting healthy estrogen levels that keep vaginal tissues supple too.

Maximise DHEA levels in the body. DHEA balances the immune system, helps to repair tissues, improves brain function and promotes healthy skin. In short, orgasms make you younger and healthier.

Release endorphins (feel-good hormones) into the body that flush out cortisol (inflammatory hormone in the flight/fight mode) from the body.

Boost by up to 20% the infection-fighting cells in our bodies.

Elevate pain thresholds (getting your body ready for childbirth) so things like migraines decrease in intensity.

Increase your oxytocin level that is not only associated with passion but also with intuition and social bonding skills. It's an all-round win!

So sex and passion are important and good.

As are their cousins: love and connection.

Love and connection: a bridge across the Fs

What is love?

The ancient Greeks called love 'the madness of the gods'. Modern psychologists define it as the strong desire for emotional union with another person, but what, actually, *is* love? It means so many different things to different people. Songwriters have described it, "Whenever you're near, I hear a symphony." Shakespeare said: "Love is blind and lovers cannot see." Aristotle said: "Love is composed of a single soul inhabiting two bodies." But technically, love is derived from one of three basic *brain systems* that evolved for mating and reproduction, comprising:

Sex drive or lust: the craving for sexual gratification. This evolved to enable you to seek a range of potential mating partners. After all, you can have sex with someone you aren't in love with. You can even tap into and activate your sex drive when you are driving in your car, reading a magazine or watching a movie. Lust is not necessarily focused on a particular individual.

Romantic love, or attraction: the obsessive thinking about and craving for a *particular* person. This evolved to enable you to focus your mating energy on just one individual at a time. As Kabir, the Indian poet, put it: "The lane of love is narrow; there is room for only one."

Attachment: the feeling of deep union with a long-term partner. This evolved to enable you to remain with a mate at least long enough to rear a single child through infancy together as a team. Today, given longevity and our modern ideas of romantic love, many of us remain together much longer and enjoy the benefits of life with a partner even when there is no goal to have children.

As you now know about the key concepts of the brain, you can recognise that love is a primeval force.

When I was looking for connection and ultimately love in the 80s, it was relatively straight forward. Dress up. Go out. Drink cocktails. Go to Xenon nightclub near Piccadilly Circus in London. Or another trendy club. Dance. Drink more. Flirt. Meet someone. Go somewhere else. Possibly go to their place or yours or just go home in a cab with your girlfriends. This was the early 80s and we, supposedly liberated feminists, were making a repeated mistake. We were equating sex with love and connection. Sure we got connection for a brief time but it led to repeat rejection and feelings of lower self-worth at times.

My innocent view about sex and all the joys, pains and potential dangers it can bring changed in 1985. I was lying sunbathing on a hot beach in Salou, Spain listening, via a transistor radio at my ear, to a Spanish station that played British pop music. "Rock Hudson esta muerto." Even with my limited grasp of Spanish, I knew what this meant. Rock Hudson is dead. Wow, Rock Hudson, hunk, movie star, lothario and heartthrob suddenly dead. How sad. I didn't realise it would be life-changing for so many. He had died of AIDS and his image of being a macho heterosexual was a necessary cover (in the movie industry of that time) for being gay.

Upon my return to London, this new fear of AIDS was gripping everyone. The government helpfully fanned the flames of panic with adverts of dark morbid tombstones crashing down into dust. Being informed and intelligent (not to mention terrified) young women, my friends and I learned that this was not, as the tabloids had so compassionately called it, 'a gay plague', but a disease that was affecting heterosexuals too. We truly believed that we were all doomed. We had had unprotected sex. We were on the pill. I'd even dated two Americans and that, according to several hysterical tabloid reports, was a death sentence. There was nothing else for it but to get checked so off we went to the, as it was still affectionately called in those days, VD clinic (hidden within a Family Planning clinic). I had hoped to catch a glimpse of musician Hank Wangford who we knew to be moonlighting as Dr Sam Hutt, a National Health Service physician at the Margaret Pyke Centre (where we chose to go, anonymously) in central London, but sadly no. Arriving for my blood test at the clinic, my only positive thought was that at least I might be examined by a minor celebrity. I went with three girlfriends. We all returned a week later for our results and sat clutching each other's hands awaiting some fatal words. Thankfully they didn't come. We were AIDS-free.

This focused us on finding 'the one' as being young free and single no longer seemed like fun. It was time to settle down. Crazy as it sounds that is exactly what we all decided. No more one night stands. Having gone through university as a feminist with a badge declaring 'A woman without a man is like a fish without a bicycle', I'd never had any imaginings about the perfect white wedding or the dress. Yet marriage was where my, and many other independent women's, thoughts and actions turned to at that time.

Having married in my late 20s and again in my early 40s I never anticipated having to join the dating scene again. For someone vibrant, intelligent, with a great life, who has come through adversity and divorced twice and is over 50, this is not an easy step.

After some resistance, I concluded that it had to be online. After all, I work mostly one-on-one with clients (not in any kind of office environment), have nights out with friends in groups or at sensible 'non pick up' places or hang out with my family.

Many girlfriends ask me this: Where do you go? Which websites are best for grown-ups? Well you have to decide why you want to be there. For me it has to be to meet someone special. I have more friends than I can see regularly, love my home and work and don't need a pen pal.

Over 15 million people in the UK are registered for online dating and one in five relationships now start online. It's the third most popular way to meet (after pubs and through friends). However, fast forward to a year's worth of online dating and watching several sobering TED talks and it seems that the failure rate, even for 'committed' relationships that start online, can be high. So is it a question of choosing the right site? With a reported 14,000 dating sites available, where do you start?

This is a vulnerable place. It is a whole new world and people naturally feel very exposed and ill at ease. When we were sipping cocktails back in the 80s and flirtily making eye contact across a bar we didn't, for a nanosecond, imagine that 30 years later we would be dating again and via the internet, opening ourselves up to complete strangers in the hope of forming a close, intimate and loving relationship. It can feel almost like the slaves being auctioned off in Spartacus – "Look at this one," Peter Ustinov cries, "his teeth are rotten. Like chalk. No good at all."

Having heard horror stories of men sending portfolio photos of their penis as some sort of wooing technique I concluded that it had to be paid for. There are sites for people over 50 such as OurTime that has recently arrived in the UK from the US. It states that: 'OurTime is a niche-dating site designed for mature singles. Anyone who is over the age of 50 can join the site and connect with other seniors looking for love or companionship'. It looks a bit like the Saga catalogue to me. I don't want to be lumped together with all the other 'fun 50s'. Definitely not for me, thanks.

Being attracted to the idea of it being 'elite' and for 'educated sophisticated singles' I took the first plunge with Elite Singles.

Elite Singles puts a lot of store in its psychometric profiling tool. Informing me that:

"Our test is currently one of the most comprehensive analyses of your personality by any online matchmaking service. Based on your input we have created your personalised profile and compared it with other Elite Singles members. This is particularly useful since it allows you to gain a better picture of what it is that makes you an individual. Based on all these key data points, we calculate a range of potential partners for you."

In addition to basic personality traits (The Big Five comprising: Conscientiousness; Agreeableness; Openness to experience;

Extroversion and Neuroticism), the test takes into account your personal interests, values and attitudes. I was wildly optimistic.

Furnished with my scores and an assessment that categorises me as extremely emotionally stable, I upload a profile and photos. I aim to be unapproachably approachable. Showcasing my intelligence and yet being open in my search for a mate.

I post smiling photos but not too much flesh. It goes live. No one responds. I edit the text down, make it more accessible, enquiries start to come through. Then in month three of my three-month sign up I totally change it, I appear light and fun and yet with integrity. More suitors come forward and I quickly move to chatting via direct email and then the phone. I strike up a good rapport with a chap from London. We meet. We have a relationship. He is adorable but after months of seeing each other, mostly at weekends, I realise I have a very good friend and not a passionate life partner. I get on the train, go to London and end it face-to-face. Not a good day out but we part as friends and wish each other well.

For several months I worked on myself again. Attended A-Fest on the theme of Love and Relationships, went to LifeBook in Barcelona, all the time aiming to work out what I wanted from a relationship. As Ester Perel shared at the workshop of hers that I attended, what we really want in a love relationship is 'intimacy' or 'Into Me See'. That deepest, most profound level of connection where the other person is able to see into you and connect at the very heart and soul of your being. So you had better be prepared. You could waste hours and emotional energy taking the personality tests, creating a great profile that invites others in, chat, speak, meet and start a relationship, and then when they look into you sadly they really don't like what they see and are gone. Leaving you rejected and as we know, rejection sucks.

The route to an amazing relationship is to become the person you want to attract. Clearly not by becoming the object of your desire but by matching their values, standards of behaviour and character.

If you want to attract someone driven, solvent, slim and fit, adventurous, intelligent, able to take risks and be open, passionate and good looking, guess what? Chances are they will want the same in their partner. It is unlikely that someone like this will hanker after a couch potato, with poor personal standards, no drive and total aversion to change and risk.

If you want them to love what they see in you then you need to look inside yourself and work out if you like what you see. Love what you see.

If you are filled with self-loathing or self-doubt then hiding it with any of the masks we wear – makeup, fine clothes, accessories, toys, cosmetic procedures, etc – may work for a while. Like a sticking plaster. It may even hold up long enough to get someone interested, but after five minutes you are on your own.

It is also crucial to determine what you want from a love relationship. Make a list. I did. Create a manifestation list of what your ideal mate would be like and look like. What are their values? What do you want? Do you want connection? Respect? To be valued? To come first in their life? Then one of the many profiles where the man says that his children come before anything and everything else in the world may start to ring an alarm bell for you. It may be just that they are trying to sound like a decent family oriented person and why not? So at an early date you have to establish just how flexible they are going to be on this one.

I was in a painful relationship (prior to internet dating) where it was made crystal clear to me that I would never come first. That his children, family and extended family of 'blood ties' would always come first and that my children (who it was helpfully pointed out were not even 'blood') and I would always be at the back of the queue. For me that is now a deal breaker. I expect each partner in a love relationship to work to put the other first or at least on an equal footing as all the existing family who are in the picture. There is enough love and respect and time to go around. Men on dating sites in particular need to think about this one. When they state: 'My wonderful children mean the world to me and will always come first', I applaud their fidelity and parenting, but what you are saying to any potential mate or life partner is, 'You will always come second... or third' and this potential relationship may wither and die due to lack of attention and nurture towards you.

Rather than a place of love and mutual respect the relationship can deteriorate into a nasty tit-for-tat battleground, or apathy. A sort of 'settling' where the thought of loneliness or finding 'the one' seems such an effort that you will just carry on as 'it's not really too bad'.

Don't live your life in 'settling' or 'not too bad'. Live your life in 'it's amazing!' This was my mantra.

So my manifestation list became precise. It was like a shopping list for a very specific man. I wrote down exactly what values I wanted and how I wanted him to be. Values included the likes of being generous, sexy, intelligent, open minded, edgy, with good integrity and a spiritual side. Physical attributes included being a silver fox, with a great smile, twinkly eyes and nice teeth. Life experiences included well travelled, retired or semi-retired from a senior role or own company, divorced or widowed and living within 50 miles of my home.

I was realistic enough to incorporate flexibility (the 80/20 rule) as it is unlikely in life that you will get every single thing. For example, the desire for him to have thick salt'n'pepper hair may not be achievable, but him being edgy, kind, generous, witty can still be had. You may need to make the unfamiliar familiar and vice versa. I married two men who had the same Christian name, were both tall (6ft 2 and 6ft 3) and born the same year. Pattern or what?! I realised that I'd never been attracted previously to shorter men. When I filled in the desirable parameters on the online dating site I lowered the desired height from 5ft 11, to 5ft 8. The same height as my dear late father. It was unfamiliar, but I decided not a deal breaker.

Having gone through this exercise, when I was asked on the online form the second time around about what I wanted in a relationship I answered: Openness, putting each other first, growth, sharing, communication, passion, connection and chemistry.

This time around, I tried Encounters Dating (*The Sunday Times*) after a friend met her rather dishy husband there. I created a more open profile description. I had new photos that showed me in a good light and again were positive and open. I had my manifestation list. I was focused. I understood that most men online are rather guarded in their profiles (not to mention awful with terrible jokey photos and answers to questions that run along the lines of "I thought I'd already answered this" or "Don't know why I have to answer this. I'm here aren't I so it's obvious what I want"). I looked beyond it. I was flexible and kind, and so when I finally opened myself to someone who

Reset! A Blueprint for a Better Life

wooed me mercilessly then had my heart broken some months later I was left very hurt, bewildered and disillusioned.

That was when I noticed that the ever insightful Ester Perel was blogging on the topic of online dating. Her observations were made about Millennials, but they held up perfectly well, in my experience, for baby boomers too. I reposted Ester's article: 'Relationship Accountability and the Rise of Ghosting' ("are the new trends of ghosting, simmering and icing increasing our acceptance of ambiguous ends?"), on my Facebook page and on a number of private FB groups.

The response was overwhelming. Both women and men came forward to speak of how they had been duped, dumped and dismayed by their online experiences. How online had somehow made normal, decent, kind behaviour seem an optional extra as it creates an environment where there is a loss of relational accountability. People go from hundreds of texts a day to nothing. People 'simmer' their potential love interests, giving them just enough encouragement and contact to keep them interested while they look around for someone better

Because the huge choice of all these singles looking for love across hundreds of dating sites has to mean that surely you can meet 'the one', so why compromise? But, in practice, this was being widely misinterpreted as meaning you didn't have to work at it, to be flexible, to be kind. To try and co-create some relationship together. Go out with them for sure. Even have sex. Even make plans, but as soon as they remind you of your ex, or have a bad day, or after that 'ping' from a new potential prettier mate comes into your inbox, you can just ice them, or ghost them: just disappear. Also, particularly with the baby boomers there is a dilemma in what most people want. On one hand they want love, connection, someone 'to come home and snuggle up to on the sofa', but they also don't want to lose their independence, self-actualisation and freedom. So it translates as this sort of text I received: "Oh I'd love to hook by and take you to lunch today on my way to an afternoon of golf. Are you free?" "Er, no. I'm working. What about tomorrow?", "No can do. Off to my friend's 60th birthday party" and so it goes on.

It is brutal and I realised that I had been on the receiving end of all those poor behaviours and had been ghosted, iced and simmered. As a therapist who had studied with Ester and as a former marketer, I saw clearly that our rampant consumerism means that we now have hundreds of options and a paradox of choice when it comes to dating and meeting the one. All the time we are asking ourselves: 'Is this the one? How do I even know you are the one? How do I know that there isn't a better one?' Like some weird dating game of *Deal or No Deal* we are trying to work out, 'Should I take the banker's offer? Or hold on as there may be a better deal in one of the yet unopened boxes?'

What I did realise is that online dating can seem fun with all the attention but turning that into a real life relationship is not easy. Understanding this was cathartic. It put it into context and stopped me blaming myself, doubting my judgment, doubting the process (online dating) and doubting that despite all the work I had done on myself and being clear about what I wanted that having a close loving relationship was not to be.

So I joined Muddy Matches. So far so good and it is still in progress. Maybe it is me, but I engaged at a deeper level from the outset with men who were much more open and vulnerable. Who seem to know what they want. Maybe it is a good name for a dating site as it is not so much about loving to get muddy as realising that we are all like that glass of muddy water, waiting for it to settle to see the clear water at the top but acknowledging that there is silt at the bottom that can be stirred up.

Regardless of outcome, what I do know is that even when you have put out your stall, it is also important to remember to enjoy the journey. Just because that special person has not been attracted into your life yet doesn't mean that your life or happiness should be put on hold in any way. Be joyful on the journey. Happiness is a choice not an external set of circumstances when all your ducks are in line. As John Lennon observed: "Life is what happens when you are busy making other plans". Make the plan to have as wonderful a life as possible now, today. Make the plan to be the very best version of you so that you love what you see inside and start that journey now.

2. Family

What is your picture of your best family relationships? More than any other aspect in your life, this area can be like an incendiary device. 'You can choose your friends and not your family' so the saying goes. True, but you can choose how to relate to your family. You can choose how to value and respect them and teach them, by quietly affirming who you are, how to respect and treat you. You will be treated how you allow yourself to be treated. So often I see clients who tell me with great distress that their mother/father/sibling treats them with total disdain or disrespect. 'My mother prefers my brother. She wanted a boy and I've always been a disappointment to her.' Very painful. Very hard to address, especially if the parent has no desire to change or to change and mend the relationship, or if they are dead and the time to make amends and build bridges has passed. The only thing you can do is change your attitude towards the situation. To become indifferent to their emotional blackmail, put downs or other negative behaviour towards you or the memory of it.

Families are curious things. The British Royal Family is called 'The Firm'. They did not get the rules of interchange right with Princess Diana, nor she with them. Yet amongst the modern royals, particularly through Prince Harry's choice of bride in Meghan Markle (a mixed-race actress, a divorced, foreign, humanitarian and generally beautiful being), family dynamics are fascinating. As in the Kennedy family. The Bush family. The Kardashians. The Osbornes. The Plantagenets. The Trump family. The Corleone family..

We watch those who are royal, or famous, or infamous, or imaginary in soaps, as the dramas and vagaries of their everyday lives are played out before us. There are more than enough books already written on the topics of families and their dynamics should you want to really immerse yourself, but let's address here for a moment the patterns of behaviour that you can reset yourself with, to make your family ties and interactions as rewarding as possible.

Ask yourself some more questions such as: What is your vision for your family and children or those you are responsible for? Do you want to see your children happy and self actualised and confident? Then berating them on a daily basis may not be the most helpful path. Ignoring them and throwing your hands in the air with exasperation as they do yet one more 'stupid' thing may feel justified, but without your guidance and good example how will they navigate this difficult maze called modern life? Have you guided them about money? About saving and investing? Living well today but planning for the future? Are you a good role model? Will they want to grow up to be like you?

What kind of relationship do you want with your siblings? It is good to remember that often in your childhood you may have all played the only roles available to you in your pressure cooker family confines and now you have grown beyond that. In a tribe there are four key roles you can adopt to add value to and thus remain within that tribe. One is a nurse: the one who nurses the babies and the sick to health. One is an A-Lister: the one who goes out and shoots the arrows to protect the tribe and provide food. One is a rebel: the one who is going to do it differently and kick against the norm. They can be a pain but also they may go out and invent fire. Then there is the sick one: the one who gets attention (and love) through needing nurture and needing attention. In larger families the additional members may create an amalgam of all these roles or just be better at a certain role than another family member.

We are cast, unwittingly, into these roles. Say, for example, your father is a total high flyer, famous perhaps? Your mother is beautiful and also high flying, or perhaps she is the 'nurse' nursing your father's ego and daily needs and yours are secondary. Your elder sibling is a rebel, doing everything possible to annoy your 'perfect' parents. The late DJ John Peel said that his daughter once got really cross with him as everything she said she was doing: getting tattoos, smoking, etc, was met with the response of 'cool' or 'go for it'. Eventually in exasperation she told him that he gave her no option to 'rebel' or do anything that annoyed him. So in your tribe, to get attention your subconscious mind may cast you in the only role you can play at that time: the sick one. The child with eczema who gets Mum's attention away from the baby or rebellious older sibling as she applies cream to the eczema, creating physical contact and giving you her undivided attention, albeit for a short while.

But now that you are in your 40s or 50s (or any other age at which you are seeking out this advice and I salute you for starting your journey now), guess what? That is no longer you. You no longer have to play those roles. You no longer have to please your parents, to get their love or approval or to rebel against them as you resent their pressure on you to be the perfect child, to have a career in law or finance or whatever they deemed sensible and 'successful'.

One of my clients, who was self-sabotaging a life-improving diet recommended by a leading nutritionist (after a private gastric bypass operation that she finally gave in to as her health was at risk), realised something profound under hypnosis and so did I. Under regression she went back to scenes, and then we pieced together the fact that the only time she could stand up for herself and annoy her cruel mother was at mealtimes by creating crazy combinations of food such as strawberry and ham and jam sandwiches. She recalled whilst hypnotised: "I eat in that unhealthy way to piss off my mother". Sadly, some 40 years later she was still trying to annoy her mother, even though her mother had been dead for years.

My client's self-sabotage was a continuation of that small meal-time rebellion that at the time was the only way she could redress some sort of balance against this unloving and domineering parent. But now, the only person she was really rebelling against and hurting was herself. She was putting her life at risk. The revelation to her was life-changing. She had put her faith in expensive gastric operations and also, having lost so much weight, had booked in for many more cosmetic procedures to take away the loose fat, but she had found no joy. Until she made this realisation. This literally (and I have the cards and tears to prove it) set her free.

3. Friends

So you have to love yourself first and then you look at your friendships. This is an important part of the 6Fs Framework.

Bear with me while I relate this story: Eddie is a grizzled war veteran who feels trapped in a meaningless life of fixing rides at a seaside amusement park. As the park has changed over the years — from the Loop-the-Loop to the Pipeline Plunge — so, too, has Eddie changed, from optimistic youth to embittered old age. His days are a dull routine of work, loneliness and regret.

Then, on his 83rd birthday, Eddie dies in a tragic accident, trying to save a little girl from a falling cart. With his final breath, he feels two small hands in his — and then nothing. He awakens in the afterlife, where he learns that heaven is not a lush Garden of Eden, but a place where your earthly life is explained to you by five people who were in it. These people may have been loved ones or distant strangers. Yet each of them changed your path forever.

One by one, Eddie's five people illuminate the unseen connections of his earthly life. As the story builds to its stunning conclusion, Eddie desperately seeks redemption in the still-unknown last act of his life: Was it an heroic success or a devastating failure? The answer, which comes from the most unlikely of sources, is as inspirational as a glimpse of heaven itself.

I've literally cut and pasted this from Mitch Albom's blurb about *The Five People You Meet in Heaven*. I was moved to read this book. Having been in a dilemma about spiritual understandings of life and an afterlife, the Universe, God and the conventional religion that had given me both comfort and frustration, I didn't know how to feel, but I'm a sucker for an exploration of things that are questioned about how our lives add meaning to this life and any other life. So I read on...

Clearly a few other people did too. At my last check this book has sold over 12 million copies in 35 languages.

So I had five in my mind, and then I learned that motivational speaker Jim Rohn proclaimed that we are the average of the five people we spend the most time with. I thought about this a lot and realised that I was really missing my late father Alan who was clearly one of the most important of my Famous Five. He was witty, generous and my true North. Only now can I laugh (with him!) that not only did he have a stroke on my birthday when I was in my 40s but also chose (having actually warned me) to die of a heart attack on my 50th birthday. Bloody ruined my holiday to Sardinia is all I can say. Not to mention left a gaping hole in my world.

Back to Jim Rohn. His assertion relates to the law of averages in that the result of any given situation will be the average of all outcomes. From memory of O-Level maths this equals the mean. All successful people (especially anyone in sales) know that you have to play the averages, that to get lots of sales you get lots of rejections. It's a numbers game.

People around us really influence our environment and thus our reactions. Let's face it, this is why oppressive regimes and terrible dictatorships put all the 'good' and 'bad' people together. I've watched the award-winning dystopian drama *The Handmaid's Tale* and not only is this true but the handmaids

Reset! A Blueprint for a Better Life

wear red and the ruling class of wives wear turquoise. Jews wore stars and then had shaved heads and striped clothing whilst the Nazi's wore power uniforms. We don't only hang out with people, we also fall in with them in how we look, feel and behave. So guess what? You may not be such an individual as you think as you are very affected by those you surround yourself with. I recall a vivid scene in *Educating Rita* – a wonderful movie by Willy Russell starring Julie Walters and Michael Caine. Rita is trying to better herself and satiate her frustrated and curious mind through education with the washed-out English professor played by Caine, but as she sits in the pub one evening, surrounded by her husband, her mother and friends, she realises that she can no longer sing the 'old' songs that hold them together, or down more drinks, or blot out the possibilities of the world she is striving to be part of. She has to surround herself with new people.

When self-help author and podcaster Tim Ferriss was asked on a book tour what he would print on a billboard if given the chance, he said: "You are the average of the five people you most associate with". As part of my LifeBook exercises I examined this and it is true. It may seem harsh but it is undeniably true. The five or so people you spend the most time with shape who you are. Those few who are closest to you have the greatest impact on your way of thinking and decisions.

As discussed, because you need to treat your life plan in the same way as a business plan, then you also need to re-evaluate who the five closest friends need to be in your life regularly. Do you have a wonderful life but many of your friends (who are fun, stimulating, great for holidaying with, etc) let you off the hook when you can't be bothered to go to the gym? Is being more physically fit really important to you this year? Then you need to think of a friend (or buddy or accountability partner if this makes it easier) to be close to this year who won't let you off the hook on this one. Someone who would prefer to meet you at the gym, or via a walk or a bike ride or whatever, rather than in the wine bar?

It was in the 90s that I first came across the concept of choosing and editing your friendship group. Up to that time it had been accidental with no intention or strategy involved at all. Some friends seemed to last the journey as I moved from broke student to early jobs, moving up the career ladder to having my own PR company and huge house in London in my early 30s. Some didn't. Envy or choosing a different path drove us apart. Some simply moved away, and in the days before Facebook hook-ups that was pretty much that as we all got on with our busy lives.

Standing in the kitchen of my friend Elaine one afternoon, she was very teary and I asked why. "Oh my friendship divorce is really hurting at the moment," she replied. "What?" I asked. "A friendship divorce?"

She explained that one of her friendships had run its course, and that this girlfriend was actually pulling her down and being a toxic influence in her life; a frenemy as it is called today. So, after much heart-searching, Elaine had met with her for coffee and explained that they were getting divorced and that their friendship was over. Wow. It seemed rather surreal.

Most people just let things slide, including friendships. So fast forward to today when we feel more valued by the amount of friends we can parade in numbers across Facebook, etc.

'Congratulations you have 250 Facebook Friends' comes the message. When I say how many Twitter followers I have, people are impressed, yet when any one of these contacts, who I don't know beyond the platform, starts to contact me in a chatty 'let's get to know each other' way via DM, I want to unfollow. Several of my girlfriends have been hit upon on Facebook and Twitter too. Delete.

It can be exhausting trying to keep up with these wide circles of friends but where do you draw the line? I have friends, particularly overseas, that I only get to see once every few years, but when we meet up we fall back into a great pattern and it feels like we saw each other only yesterday. We have a connection and it is lovely.

Do I have a rule that says: 'Anyone I don't see every year is an ex-friend'? Some people do. Many advocate it. A regular overhaul, a Friendship Spring Clean to only keep a number close and then a few more at a slight remove. Like a pebble in a pond they see the inner circle as those five or so friends of influence. People who will help you grow, hold you accountable, be your mentors, role models, cheerleaders. Then the next circle has more who are your 'tribe'. I'm taking a longer, wider view to be honest.

I belong to several tribes: A-Fest, graduates from my therapy courses, women's networking groups, mentoring groups, coaching groups, special interest groups, etc. Many are virtual (Facebook secret or members only groups or LinkedIn groups where like-minded people come together). Many are in real life, such as my Athena network or other meet ups, and they happen on a regular basis and it takes some time, money and effort to fly to meet up with them and often I do, but it is all about how you choose to spend your time, money and effort after all.

I believe that personal growth is constant, never ending and I want to spend time, as much time as possible, with like-minded people who will challenge me to grow and learn and develop. I also want to be connected to people, mostly women to be honest, who support me. Women working from home groups that make being a writer and therapist not quite so isolating.

And as for divorces? Well I've put enough time, effort and energy into two love relationship divorces so I personally don't need the drama of 'friendship' divorces. However, I do now review those two inner circles rippling out from me with more scrutiny than ever before on a quarterly basis. Have I had any contact from that friend? Is it all one way from me to them? What are my current life and career and love goals? Which of the inner circle of five or so friends should I spend more time with and effort with to help me achieve them and be the best me I can be? Are there some friends who don't meet this criterion but are just such fun to be around that I should seek them out more? Get out of my head more. Just have a laugh with? Would more effort and less judgment from me make it better for us both? I've found this to be true and I benefitted greatly as now I do at least make conscious decisions about this. I may allow myself more flexibility in my choices and who stays in my extended tribe but that is a conscious decision too.

Sometimes I just decide not to decide. To park it for a while, but I set a timeframe for any such decision and come back to it without fail. I don't live inside my life and my friendships as if it were just an accident and someone else is in the driving seat. I can offer tough love to my sons and young relatives sometimes. When I hear the mantra of: "It wasn't my fault, I didn't choose it, it just happened", I will reply along the lines of: "You are the

Reset! A Blueprint for a Better Life

boss of you. If you choose not to make a decision and shut your eyes while driving the car, that is your life, and you hit a brick wall then that was a choice, not a great one, but a choice. Let's talk together to see what we can learn from this and how to avoid hitting a brick wall in future, shall we?" As Freud said: "There are no mistakes." It is all cause and effect. That is why we have the term Freudian slip when you 'accidentally' say the wrong thing. From personal experience with my clients this is usually from a subconscious place. For example, someone explaining how they are having conflict at home may mean to say to me: "and I'm feeling very shut out by my wife" but say: "and I'm feeling very shut out by my mother". Even if their mother has been dead for many years.

Also, sometimes I have learned that my sons don't want to always come round to 'good advice'. Sometimes they want to come round to a hot dinner, a box set and love. Balance is key.

So once you are clear on your inner and outer circles of friendships, how do you maintain good relations with those you want to keep near and dear? Well, first and foremost to have friends you need to be a friend. Ask yourself: "Am I a good friend. Would I want me as a friend? Do I do some of the heavy lifting in this relationship and put myself out for that person? What do I expect from my close friends? Do they get that from me?"

It may not always be totally equal. Your chosen friend may be the challenging one that asks you the difficult questions that keep making you grow and they don't need the same in return. They want a friend who allows them to let themselves be vulnerable and 'seen'. Perhaps that is your quid pro quo with them.

The primary friendship you must focus on is you. Are you a friend to yourself? More than that, do you love and accept yourself for who you are? Have you stopped that inner monkey mind chatter of negative self-talk and harsh and hurtful criticism? The sort of words that if you said them to a friend would definitely lead to a friendship divorce? Do you set time aside for your loved ones, your friends and just for you? Can you put yourself first and not call it selfish but essential?

Those values you want from others, how well do they reside in you? If you want openness, reliability, fun, truth, compassion, grit, sensuality, compassion, empathy, joy, growth, determination or the values you hold dear from your love, family and friendship connections, how much do you embody them? To use a clichéd phrase, do you walk your talk?

Change and healing only happen when you can come to a sincere and heartfelt appreciation of all of your life experiences, even the unpleasant and painful ones, and see how they have led you to being who you are today. To move beyond this will need work. You have to set those life visions and goals and then work on the inner you.

For starters, write a letter to your younger self. It is really cathartic and can heal an inner part of you that you carry around with you every day. Like the exercise with the child in you, you can become your own loving parent. You can share the wisdom you have today and allow your inner self to know that even the struggles were not in vain and that you were never alone.

Choose a younger you at a time that was difficult. Be clear about how old the younger you that you are writing to is. Be real and authentic and drill down to a few really specific lessons or topics that you wish your younger you had known or felt at a heart level at that time. This isn't a shopping list or a way to put pressure on that former you. Be kind, imagine that younger you as you would a dearly loved younger member of your family. Imagine that you are gently holding your younger self by the shoulder as you speak to them. Use 'you' and the present tense.

Here is the starter of a letter to my 25-year-old self. At the time I was working in Dewsbury at a company I didn't like, living alone during the week in a bedsit in Headingly Leeds, with no phone and ticking off the days until I returned to my shared house in London. Increasingly I found that when I got back to London my friends would have gone away for a fun weekend. The sense of failure and isolation was so great that I felt suicidal at times and lonely pretty much all the time. It was a very difficult nine months of my life.

Dear Ros

I want you to take five minutes, sit down, breathe deeply and remember that you are a wonderful, heartfelt young woman.

What seems like a fork in the road now will lead to greater opportunities. You have courage in spadesful and do twice what most people do in half the time but remember you are a human being and be kind to yourself. Don't beat yourself up for your choices or feel life is hard and unfair. Do not allow yourself at this time to feel depressed or that life isn't worth living. It is. I promise.

You are very sensitive and vulnerable but wear such an effective mask that others often see you as impenetrable and totally in control. They even try to pull you down because of it. Know now that daring to show your vulnerability and to be open to others, to stop judging yourself and others by impossible levels of perfectionism, will be the greatest and kindest gift you can ever give yourself.

Know that you are more than enough and that your intellect and emotional intelligence will take you further than you can ever imagine so you don't need to worry about striving for success. The less you try, the more successful you will be. When you trust your inner intuition and tap into your inner power you will not just make the right choices but intuitively take the right action at the right time.

Do not let those who are afraid of your light try to dim it. You are a maverick. You see things differently and do things differently and that, coupled with your great sense of compassion, will make the world a better place.

You are curious, so remember that questions are the answer. Do not be afraid to ask questions, seek a better path, do not be a lemming and follow the herd to fit in, even if this makes others uncomfortable. Yours is a path to change the world and this will not always be comfortable to you or others. Treat their fear with grace and understanding.

Smile. People will always love you for it.

Find out what makes you happy and pursue it every day. Feel at ease with this as all that you need is already within you. Enjoy the journey. Even the bumpy roads will give you a new level of wisdom. Know that you do have a spiritual gift and will experience events, insights and visions that others will try to rubbish. Don't let them. Trust yourself.

Learn to let go. It makes skiing, sex and so much more really wonderful. Speaking of which, don't confuse sex for love or see the need for human contact and connection as anything other than sacred and wonderful. Use your body and value your body as you would worship a goddess. Remember you are more powerful, sexy, physical and sensual than you could ever know. Do not let sexual shaming or guilt diminish this either. Sex is like breath itself and vital and wonderful.

Know your worth. This is true for finding your future life partner, work, friends and all other connections. For many years you will be the power behind the throne. Notice now that much of the fame and fortune of those around you has been in part created by you. If you want to enjoy that or step into the limelight too then do not feel restricted or not good enough. Do for yourself what you do for others.

Pay close attention to your health and finances. Know that to be wealthy you need a balance of faith, fitness, friends, family, finance and forgiveness and be mindful to keep that balance always. Learn to meditate and be present.

It is not your job to make everyone around you happy, or kind or fulfilled. That is their journey. You are not a cash cow for others. Earning money and providing for your future family is not your sole responsibility. Do not sacrifice your health or happiness for success.

Trust that you know what is right for you. Create great and healthy and nurturing habits.

Understand that you studied for an English Literature degree because you feel things deeply, enjoy time alone

*and have a connection to all that is real and true
in this world. Write your own books and share your
wisdom sooner rather than later. It will just flow from
you as you tap into something even beyond your present
understanding. You are meant to be this messenger and
change agent but you are not supposed to compromise
your own happiness or health for it.*

*Only connect. Understand that people who need people
really are the happiest people of all. We are all in this
together.*

*There is so much more I could share but you know that
you will be more than OK, more than enough. You will
shine and grow and love and be loved and your life will
enrich others. Feel that and love it.*

*Oh yes and have intimacy with yourself. It means Into
Me See.*

*I see into you and I'm so excited by it, moved by it, in
love with it. Yaba daba doo!*

*Love always
56-year-old Rosalyn xx*

This exercise is often seen in magazines and newspaper weekend
supplements when a celebrity is asked to complete something
such as: 'If I knew then what I know now, I would have...'

It is rather like those moments in *Back to the Future* or *Freaky
Friday* when realising (as you have gone back in time) that
investing in the Beatles (or holding onto your rather run-
down house in Notting Hill Gate, London) would be such an
amazingly good idea.

Oh yes. I've made a few decisions that, could I go back in time and change, I would do very differently. For example, the time my office was near the startup company Innocent Smoothies. They would put jugs of their tester smoothies in the basement restaurant in my office building in the mid-90s and I loved them immediately, but I didn't respond to their request for seed capital investment. Or when I was persuaded to sell our eight-bedroom house in central London in 2001 due to an impending property 'downturn'. Where is the DeLorean? Driver please!

So, feeling better about your choices than mine I hope. Let's do something great. Close your eyes for a moment.

In your mind's eye, I want you to go back to the home that you lived in when you were six to eight years old. If that wasn't a happy place, imagine where you would have loved to live at that time. You are six, it can be a castle or under the sea. Make it fun and safe for you.

Go up the drive or stairs or dive into it and see it how it was or how you want to imagine it. Walk to your bedroom or safe place. Open the door or enter and see the younger you sitting on the bed that you slept in or where you slept at night. Sit down next to your younger self then take them in your arms and give them the most tender embrace imaginable. Just as you would your own children or grandchildren if you have them or as you would imagine that to be.

Now look into their lovely eyes and tell them: "I am now your loving parent. You are safe with me. No-one can do this like me as I'm part of you and you are part of me. I will never leave you. I will never judge you. I will always be there for you and now I'm going to tell you some important things that will increase your joy in life and let you avoid many hurts."

© Marisa Peer RTT Training Material

Now open your eyes and write the letter to your younger self. Don't review it. Just let it pour out of you.

Start with 'Dear amazing younger me. You cannot even imagine how wonderful you are now, and now you will start to understand it as I tell you...' then tell them all the wonderful things about them:

Their resilience, their ability to come back from adversity, to reinvent themselves. Their capacity for love and caring and nurture. The wonderful things they are capable of... tell them what to stop doing or never do in the first place. The things that they did to please others, the learned behaviours that they just accepted, the criticisms from teachers or parents or other unkind people that they let in, the lies about themselves that they believed as they didn't know any better. Debunk them all. Give them that advice as you remember you are holding that precious child in your arms and you are now their loving parent and protector. Just let it flow and flow and flow.

You can fast forward and give that younger you a glimpse of events to come. Important life-changing events, and give them the tools and advice to navigate these even if they were choppy waters at the time. Use the address 'you' and speak directly to your younger self. Use the sort of words and compassionate tone you would use with a child or teenager or young adult of the age you are addressing yourself. Be kind and empathetic. Be your own most loving parent ever.

Be real. Be generous with yourself as you offer advice about how to steer through life and how to take positives away from any and all life lessons however painful they were in the past. As they are in the past. You are reviewing your life, not reliving it. You can objectively give yourself the compassionate mature advice that would have helped you, comforted you at all your life stages, and overland and through and out the other side of all your life lessons.

When you are finished, close the letter with love and light, and feel lighter as you have finished this important exercise before you lighten any lingering hurts with another important 'F': Forgiveness.

4. Forgiveness

Game of Thrones is my guilty pleasure for TV viewing. I've watched every season of a programme that was one of the few things I could watch together with my son and my then step-son and that gripped me with a story that would have been worthy of Shakespeare. Houses Stark of Winterfell; Tully of Riverrun; Arryn of the Eyrie; Baratheon of Storm's End; Tyrell of Highgarden; Martell of Dorne and others including Greyjoy of Pyke, rulers of the Iron Islands fight each other in terrible ways as they seek to win over the seven kingdoms. There is not much mercy shown to each other's enemies in any episode. New and increasingly cruel punishments abound. Despite this darkness there are characters who are essentially at the centre of light and hope. No-one, given the circumstances they are in, is 100% good, but many of the Stark family, the rather wonderful Brienne of Tarth, the conflicted Tyrion Lannister, Samwell Tarly and central character Jon Snow, all win in the good vs evil count, but they are in short supply.

Similarly, the mafia may well believe that "Revenge is a dish best served cold. With a long handled spoon", but I've seen how those movies pan out, and *The Sopranos*. However far you are away from an act of revenge you will hold it in your heart. Many may pretend that it doesn't damage them but as a therapist I beg to differ. Hardly a day goes by when I don't see the terrible price people pay for not letting go of past hurts. As another saying goes: "Holding on to anger or resentment is like drinking poison and expecting the other person to die."

Forgiveness is key. For some people and many clients I've worked with, the shift to forgiving a parent or adult for unspeakable behaviour towards them may just not be within their gift. They may still truly hate the person and often rejoice that they are dead or living a life of misery. They may be angry and hurt that this perpetrator seems to have got away 'scot-free' while they, the victim, continue to suffer.

I'm a therapist not a priest. It is not my job to force anyone to forgive any other person, apart from one. Themselves. They have to forgive themselves for 'allowing it to happen'. They have to forgive themselves for carrying around this cup of poison and sipping from it for years and years and possibly really compromising their life, their happiness, their health. They have to let go.

They can often forgive the 'acts' that were perpetrated against them by seeing with objective eyes that it was not their fault and that the perpetrator was weak or damaged themselves or is now possibly suffering badly. Marisa Peer says: "Our punishment and reward in life are the same." The only person you go to bed with and wake up with every day for your whole life is you. At a deep level, even the seemingly tough gangster knows what he has done or, if still in denial, is paying a price for it.

Take the movie *Analyze This*. The character of mob boss Paul Vitti (played by Robert De Niro) is losing his grip as the nefarious world he occupies and a drive-past killing of his friend have prompted panic attacks. He secretly seeks out psychiatric help, confiding in his wingman Jelly who recommends Ben Sobel (played by Billy Crystal). At first Vitti can't even admit it is he who is seeking the help and says: "Hey doc, I have a friend who ...' Dr Sobel isn't fooled and says: "I'm going out on a limb here but I think that your friend is you." "You are good," comes the reply and then Dr Sobel finds he has a client who does not understand the word 'no'. When Vitti wants therapy he expects to get it, even following Dr Sobel on his honeymoon in order to get a face-to-face consultation.

It is a black comedy but ultimately Vitti has to let go of the guilt and burdens of his actions.

The concept of Radical Forgiveness is very powerful. In a Christian context, the most powerful example I have come across is from Rwanda. Here is an extract from *As We Forgive: Stories of Reconciliation from Rwanda* by Catherine Claire Larson who gathered her research while working for Prison Fellowship Ministries. There was a particular problem in Rwanda in so much as too many people needing to be guarded, judged, rehabilitated, etc, were in jail. How do you let them out when those whose families they slaughtered are back in their communities? Says a review of Larson's book:

"What does forgiveness really look like? How can you forgive someone who seemingly took everything away that made life worth living: family, homes and trust? What kind of power is it that can look someone who has hurt you in the deepest way and forgive them? This is what As We Forgive is about, specifically how do Rwandan survivors of the 1994 genocide forgive those who broke into their homes, chased them down in the wild and sought to wipe them out.

"The 1994 Rwandan genocide, where Hutu attacked and murdered over 800,000 Tutsi's is hard to fathom in its brutality and suddenness. By telling personal stories in an engaging writing style, Larson does a fine job of taking the reader from the abstract to the very real and personal. She only introduces the political issues that motivated the genocide and steps out of the way to tell of very human stories of brutality and in return peace and reconciliation.

"If you were told that a murderer was to be released into your neighborhood, how would you feel? But what if it weren't only one, but thousands? Could there be a common roadmap to reconciliation? Could there be a shared future after unthinkable evil? If forgiveness is possible after the slaughter of nearly a million in a hundred days in Rwanda, then today, more than ever, we owe it to humanity to explore how one country is addressing perceptual, social-psychological and spiritual dimensions to achieve a more lasting peace. If forgiveness is possible after genocide, then perhaps there is hope for the comparably smaller rifts that plague our relationships, our communities and our nation. Based on personal interviews and thorough research, As We Forgive returns to the boundary lines of genocide's wounds and traces the route of reconciliation in the lives of Rwandans — victims, widows, orphans and perpetrators — whose past and future intersect. We find in these stories how suffering, memory and identity set up roadblocks to forgiveness, while mediation, truth-telling, restitution and interdependence create bridges to healing. As We Forgive explores the pain, the mystery and the hope through seven compelling stories of those who have made this journey toward reconciliation. The result is a narrative that breathes with humanity and is as haunting as it is hopeful."

You may not reach radical forgiveness as you may just never be able to feel that those who hurt you truly deserve it. My great uncle Ray, who had been a Japanese prisoner of war, would never buy a Japanese car or appliance until the day he died. I stopped going to a celebrity hairdresser in London in the 90s as he berated me (whilst cutting my hair one day) for what the English had done to the Scots after watching the movie *Braveheart*. I felt compassion for the hurt. I was as outraged as he was at the injustices of history, but I didn't see why I had to be berated just because I'd been born in the UK. I didn't even bother to talk about my lineage back to Ireland and the time of the potato famine. Just let it go, and his salon too. I'm not sure if I'd react the same today. I do think that some redress has to be made for some historic wrongs yet it's hard when you are being held accountable for the sins of your forefathers. Compassion and forgiveness on both sides I feel is needed.

It may be true that the perpetrator does not deserve forgiveness in your eyes but you deserve to see the world through better eyes. Not one's clouded by the mist of anger or resentment or hatred. If you keep sipping that cup of poison and stumbling blindly on, guess what happens? It is you who will pay the biggest price as you compromise your life, your happiness, and your health. It may take intervention and guidance from a third party, a therapist or other to enable you to let go but that is your goal. That must be your goal. For your sake.

When the cancer came I had a vivid dream.

Leading up to that time my father had had a stroke and got very depressed. I was displaced, in a foreign country with two young adopted children who had many needs and many previous hurts. I had lost my identity. My home. My friends.

My sense of self. My family felt a long, long way away. I felt like an alien in the world I inhabited yet with grit had embraced it, made friends, involved myself in charity work, tried to love this new world.

The cancer changed that. It changed everything.

The dream had me clinging onto the edge of a steep parapet on a cliff in blinding rain and a howling wind. It was dark and the dark chasm of the void stretched out below me. I was clinging on with my finger tips and someone kept stepping on them, making me loosen my grip. I struggled and struggled and then words, as clear as if someone were standing at the side of me, commanded me to 'Let go'.

And I did. I awoke with a sense of perfect calm, serene surrender, and then navigated the cancer journey and all the other things that life threw at me in the upcoming year with a sense of spiritual and emotional calm. Cancer treatment overseas. Calm. No one to look after my children while I needed to travel overseas for treatment. Calm. Dad deteriorating. Calm. A house move. Calm. Already unsettled children unsettled more. Mostly calm. Two hurricanes. Calm (but exhausted). Mum's terminal cancer diagnosis. Not too calm. Very angry with God. Finding out about personal financial loss. Not quite so calm. Divorce. Painful, but I survived. The Weeble wobbled and didn't fall down. Instead, I grew. That voice in my head kept reminding me to 'let go'. Sometimes it is all you can do. It is never too late. The life beyond it, lived with conscious intelligence and awareness, is worth it. Trust me.

I worked with a wonderful client who had had a business and properties and lost the former to an unscrupulous business partner and the latter to the economic downturn in his country.

He had turned to alcohol to numb the pain and the rage. It was about to ruin his life. His wife was at the end of her tether. His grown-up children were inviting him round less and less. He didn't speak to his siblings any more. His health was severely compromised. It took several sessions to really get him to let go, as we discovered together through hypnotherapy that he felt that if he let go, it would be an admission that he could have done so 10 years earlier and had blighted the last decade needlessly.

Only through realising how not letting go at this juncture would play out across the next decade and future, pacing himself to what ultimate price he would pay for the ticket to every bottle of spirit available, did he finally let go. He was able to see the positives of the last 10 years and how the experiences had allowed him to arrive at this moment, the moment he could finally let go and reclaim his life so that the next 10, 20, 30 years would be the best they could be. That he would be the best 'he' he could be and improve all the 6Fs in his life: his fitness; his faith (in himself); his family relationships; his friendships; his finances; his fun. He was able to forgive himself and let go.

You may come home one day, after 30 years of marriage, the kids having got through university or found their passions, just as you and your partner are about to segue into the semi-retirement idyll that you have been planning for, to find a letter propped against the salt shaker telling you that your partner has left you. Bam! Like that.

Undeniably, such a split in later life can at first feel devastating. You need to mourn it. Mourn the future you had envisioned. Mourn the past you had cherished. Mourn that togetherness. Those promises. That hope. Mourn the fact that your trust has been temporarily broken. Treat the shock and the sense of loss with as much compassion and seriousness as if it were a true bereavement because it is really. Reach out to family and friends for help and support. Focus on the other Fs too. Get your finances in order, take advice and guidance, especially if this was not one of the areas you focused on in your previous relationship. Prioritise your health. Eat well. Sleep well, and don't allow yourself to get medicated up to the eyeballs with sleeping tablets and antidepressants. It took me years to come off mine. Zopiclone and Citalopram were my crutches on and off for seven years. Never again.

See an acupuncturist or herbalist for natural ways to help sleep. Seek therapy to deal with the anger. Create new routines and rituals not just at bedtime but during the day. Create peace and calm in your house. Declutter it. Remove traces of your partner as soon as you are sure that the situation is not fixable while playing the song from South Pacific, *I'm going to wash that man right out of my hair* loudly. (Clearly change it to woman if you are male.)

Above all be kind to yourself. You don't need to tell or explain the split to anyone or everyone. It is just exhausting.

Find a good car mechanic, handyman, gardener, cook or whatever tasks your partner used to do well, or enlist for a course at U3A or similar to learn these skills or new skills. Always fancied pottery? Go for it.

Above all rediscover, or perhaps for the first time ever discover, who you are. Don't rush into someone else's arms until you have done the heavy lifting on yourself. Until you have let go of the hurts. Until you have become your own best friend and are able to fill yourself with love.

Reset! A Blueprint for a Better Life

5. Finance

I recall an Oprah show. She was discussing money, and the one thing that stuck in my mind was her repetition of 'Write your own cheques'. We may not use cheques much anymore but the message still stands and it is about taking control of and an interest in your finances. I took my eye off the ball for many years (admittedly due to many other pressing external factors such as the cancer) and discovered to my horror that much of my hard-earned money had gone. I had money blocks before I had hypnotherapy and then went on to earn millions. Many of my clients have money blocks, or self-sabotage when they start to earn well. The underlying reasons can be myriad but invariably they will be to do with attitudes towards money that surrounded you when you were growing up.

Here is an exercise for you. Take out a clean piece of paper and write down, quickly, for about five minutes, everything that you believe about money or heard about money when you were growing up. This will include things such as:

- Money doesn't grow on trees
- Money is the root of all evil
- I can make money but never keep money
- If I am rich, I won't be a spiritual or decent person

And so on. Whatever is right for you. Just pour it out onto the paper.

Now. Take the list and strike a line through each word associated with money, such as 'money' or 'wealth' or 'rich'. Then replace them all with the word 'energy'.

Exercise: © Marisa Peer RTT Training Material

So now your list will read something like:

- However hard I work I will never have enough energy
- People with energy are evil
- You have to save energy for a rainy day

Etc.

Notice how different that feels as you read the amended list. It even seems ludicrous, doesn't it?

By understanding that money and the exchange of money (for goods or services, reciprocity indeed) is as natural a flow of energy and exchange of energy as a river flowing to the sea. As blood flowing around your body.

Only by letting this energy flow can you grow. Energy flows where attention goes and this is very true of money. By being open to money and wealth, letting it flow to you and through you, you pass that energy on and give it to others. You see money as a force for good. Think of all the good you can do with it. People would not have jobs if you didn't buy their goods or services. Any money excess to your real needs can be given to others and you can become altruistic and helpful to those less fortunate than yourself. No longer do you need to fill yourself up with spending needlessly on things that you don't need. It is all in perfect balance and harmony.

Then take some tangible steps to get into flow with money. Speak to a financial advisor, accountant or estate planner to make the most of the money and resources you have and plan ahead for your future earnings. Link your vision of your future – the house and lifestyle you want – to what that would cost? I've undertaken this exercise several times and been surprised by the fact that an amount for financial freedom is not as high

Reset! A Blueprint for a Better Life

as you might guess. There are several books and programmes to help you assess this level and create a blueprint for financial freedom. I've worked through Financial Mastery with Tony Robbins, and the category on money in LifeBook.

What I learned is to take two immediate steps each time I re-evaluate my financial situation and plan financial freedom. Firstly, work out how much you are currently spending. Track it for a few months and then divide the spend between wants and needs. Even the needs, such as heating, etc, may need a review, as a switch to a new supplier could save you money. There are so many wonderful customer advice sites like moneyexpert.com in the UK that can help you here.

Then evaluate how much cash you have coming in and work out the difference between money/income in and money/expenditure out. The key is to make this a positive number, and once you have that, to work out how to make it work harder for you or become bigger. Obviously if you have, for example, £10,000 in cash (savings) and an income of £3,000, then you have just over three months until you are broke. That is how a company, particularly a charity, is judged. Does it have a buffer of at least three months? This now gives you some freedom to plan, possibly retrain, etc. You know that at any time you have three months of freedom and it may be that you need that time, as a sabbatical, for example, to do everything advisable in this book and reset your life across all its categories while being very focused on planning a new financial future. Part of this will be your new mindset, getting away from your reptilian brain that resists change and activates the fear response of 'don't do anything that could harm you'. But reassuring yourself and your brain that you have a period of three months (or whatever your freedom buffer is) to work out a new and better future will allow your brain and your amygdala (your reptilian brain) to relax and let you vision, plan and execute without panic or procrastination.

Reset!

Whatever you need to Reset: your faith in yourself of life; your friendships and connections; your family relationships; your fitness in body and mind (and soul); your finances and financial future; your ability to forgive – starting with yourself; your right to have fun; JFDI (Just Fucking Do It!).

Just:

Re-read this book.

Review what was good about your life.

Remember to write to your younger self.

Relive the good.

Replace the bad.

Re-envision the future.

Re-engineer yourself to find joy in every moment and every environment.

Relax.

Reward yourself for the road travelled so far.

Revel in the new you. You are worth it!

To the journey.

Postscript

The title speaks of a blueprint for a better life. This includes joy. I want more of it. I'm sure you want more of it too. I wondered what joy meant to different people so asked the question publicly and here are some of the responses:

"When my grandbaby looks in my eyes and then lays his head on my shoulder."

"When my agent calls to say I'm booked."

"That feeling of being alive, like a breath of fresh air."

"When I head out on my motorbike (50+ woman)."

"When I'm truly living my life in gratitude, I am also experiencing joy. It's an exhilarating feeling that all things are as they are meant to be."

"The joy of running my business: the business of my dreams."

"Playing out in the woods with my three and five year olds; discovering bugs, digging up rocks, climbing trees. Nothing better."

"Awe and wonder; young children experience this in bucketloads and then it gets lost in the human noise of being busy."

"I use the word JOY daily. Joy is high vibration, feels like flying, feels like I am outside myself giggling."

"Joy for me is the feeling of lightness, no negativity, everything is fine, at ease and I get it, just like when I dance."

"Joy is the ecstasy, the pleasure, the growth, the still, the simple, the sunshine, the other side of pain, the laughter, the smell of jasmine and new babies, the quiet, the deep contentment, the new, the old, the fleeting, the forever connection to the self, connection to another, connection to nature, connection to the source. Everything is joy. I am joy!"

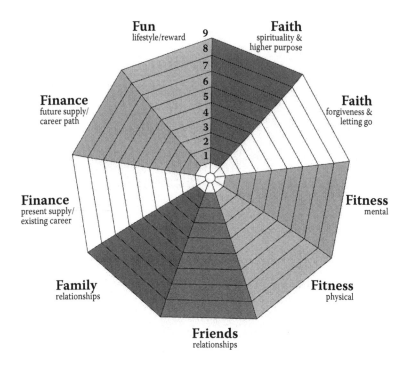

Books, individuals and resources mentioned

Lisa Nichols **https://www.motivatingthemasses.com**

Sonia Choquette **https://soniachoquette.net**

JJ Virgin **https://jjvirgin.com**

Tony Robbins UPW **https://www.tonyrobbins.com/events/ unleash-the-power-within/**

Ellen Langer **http://www.ellenlanger.com/home/**

Rhonda Byrne **https://www.rhondabyrne.com**

John Assaraf **http://johnassaraf.com**

Ester Perel **https://www.estherperel.com**

Marisa Peer **https://www.marisapeer.com/books/**

Bob Proctor **http://www.proctorgallagherinstitute.com**

Jack Canfield **http://www.thesuccessprinciples.com**

Marci Shimoff **http://happyfornoreason.com/about-marci/**

LifeBook **http://mylifebook.com**

A-Fest **https://www.afest.com**

Bulletproof coffee **https://blog.bulletproof.com/bulletproof-for-beginners/**

Xpill **https://www.xpill.com**

Belleruth Naparstek **https://www.healthjourneys.com**

Dr. Joseph Mercola **https://www.mercola.com**

Juicy Oasis **https://www.juicyoasis.com**

Linda Booth **https://www. justfortummies.co.uk**

Further reading

I read self-improvement books regularly and have shelves full. This list is my 'go to' selection of books I tend to recommend or read repeatedly:

Daring Greatly **Brené Brown**

Mating in Captivity **Ester Perel**

You Can Be Thin **Marisa Peer**

The Celestine Prophecy **James Redfield**

The Way of The Peaceful Warrior **Dan Millman**

Awaken The Giant Within **Tony Robbins**

A Return To Love **Marianne Williamson**

The Journey **Brandon Bays**

The Biology of Belief **Bruce Lipton**

The Seven Habits of Highly Effective People **Stephen R. Covey**

Who Moved My Cheese? **Ken Blanchard and Spencer Johnson**

Rich Dad Poor Dad **Robert Kiyosaki**

The Prophet **Kahlil Gibran**

The Five People You Meet in Heaven **Mitch Albom**

The Thoughtful Leader: How to use your head and your heart to inspire others **Mindy Gibbins-Klein**

© Ursula Kelly @Ursulakphoto

About the author

Rosalyn Palmer is a Master Rapid Transformational Therapist/ Clinical Hypnotherapist, RTT Trainer and Coach with proven success in addressing issues, particularly for baby boomer women, for lasting, positive change. She works worldwide via Zoom and is a member of the National Council of Psychotherapists, General Hypnotherapy Register and Complementary & Natural Healthcare Council.

Rosalyn is also a broadcaster and newspaper columnist and a regular contributor to a number of online publications writing on the issues of health and wellbeing.

She is a guest lecturer at Nottingham Trent University.

Rosalyn writes with honesty and draws on her wealth of personal experience with a background in running an award-winning PR company in London, journalism, marcomms for international charities and her many life challenges including cancer, divorce, loss of identity and wealth, country moves, re-invention of career, depression, crossing class barriers and reinventing herself. As the 'power behind the throne' for many celebrities, royalty, leading CEOs and leading PD experts, she gained massive insight into their lives and philosophies.

She lives in the UK with her cats, surrounded by friends and love.

For more information, go to:

rosalynpalmer.com

twitter @rosalynpalmer

Facebook: @RosalynPalmerTrustTransformation

LinkedIn: www.linkedin.com/in/rosalynpalmer

https://medium.com/@RosalynPalmer

Notes

Notes

Notes

Notes

Notes

Notes

Printed in Great Britain
by Amazon

86548644R00120